Sink or Swim: Tales From the Deep End of Everywhere

BRENDA KELLEY KIM

Copyright 2016 Brenda Kelley Kim
All Rights Reserved
ISBN: 1532743076
ISBN 13: 9781532743078

DEDICATION

If you are very lucky, there is someone you know who always says, "You can do it. Don't you ever give up." This book is for that person. A faithful anam cara, whose voice may only have whispered but never once wavered and who remained steadfast in the belief that I could do this. Thank you. Fluctuat nec mergitur

---BKK

ACKNOWLEDGMENTS

"Individually, we are one drop. Together, we are an ocean.

----*Ryunosuke Satoro*

This book would not have been possible without a boatload of people who gave me their time, their expertise and their advice but most importantly their love and friendship. First and foremost: my family. Not everyone gets what it's like to live with a writer, but you all did a spectacular job of it. Children, even my exceptionally bright and precious snowflakes, don't always understand what it means when Mom is staring at a computer screen for hours on end. Thank you Andy, George and Devin for understanding why the office door was closed a lot and dinner was often out of a greasy bag or a cereal box. You three are the reason I get up in the morning, and probably part of the reason I go to bed every night bleary-eyed and mumbling to myself. I wouldn't have it any other way though. You made me a mother, something no one else could have done. It's been some kind of wonderful. To my brother, and his beautiful family, you showed me what patience and dedication can do and I remain in bewildered awe of the way you all work together.

To my friends, I owe a debt that can never be repaid, but the good part is that real friends don't ever expect anything in return. Friendship is best when given freely, and I am lucky to have so many of you with me on this crazy road. Big huge thanks go to Rosemary, Kristen, Trish, Catherine, Mandy, the other Mandy, Wendy, Barb, Mike, Ulrike and too many others to list here. My wine glass runneth over, but to you all I say "Slainte"

To Mary, my friend from a thousand wars, who never hesitated to open her home, her heart and a box of chocolates for me, there are almost no words to say how grateful I am. So much of this book happened at her vintage, diner-esque Formica table and chairs. She's been to a combat zone and witnessed the birth of my daughter, two experiences that were more similar than you'd think. She's surfaced out of the deep end time and again with grace and dignity. She remains the one person who always says, "I think that's wonderful" when I have an idea.

To my badminton friends, the Mavens of Monday Mornings, who gave me this addicting game and a place to work out my frustrations, thank you, thank you, a thousand times thank you. You will always be in my heart.

To the many women that I know from my online pursuits, you are more than real to me. There is nothing that's imaginary about the support you've shown and the good times we have had. To the RGL, the Vagabonds and all the other Facebook peeps, thank you for giving me so much material.

To Kris Olson my first editor at the Marblehead Reporter and later his capable successor Chris Stevens, thank you for giving me space in the paper and in your calendar and for always having my back. Editors can sometimes be a thorn in the side of writers and writers often annoy editors, but working with you both made me better than I ever thought I could be. Each week you shepherded me through topics, quotes, grammar and even hate mail and you did it with class and humor. Will Dowd, you are a gifted journalist but mostly you are my rock for listening to all my petty squabbles and complaints.

To Kristin Nyberg for your spectacular artwork and vision and to Nancy Davis Merrey, Kristen Marsh Cunningham and LeeAnne Pantuso Clark (or LAC as she will always be known) for your capable editing, tech help and attention to detail you have my deepest appreciation and thanks. You all answered the call and gave me so much more than I could have expected.

1

"Clutter is not just the stuff on your floor---it's anything that stands between you and the life you want to be living."

----Peter Walsh

The "Big O" is a huge deal for me. There are books about it, in the self-help section naturally. They make all kinds of tools to help me get there, and it seems like everyone has their own theory about how it should be done. At least once a week someone offers me a tip about some new creative way for me to stay on top of what matters for as long as it takes to get me there. While there have been times when it's been deliciously close, still the sweet flow of it eludes me. Organization, that is. What did you think I meant? Please, get your minds out of the gutter.

Staying organized is a struggle for me, but other people I know seem to glide through their days, getting things done and being in control of all the moving parts. Their ducks are always in a row. My ducks are lost; they flew south and haven't been heard from since. Perhaps my organized friends were just born that way? Could it be a congenital thing that you either have or don't have?

I hit the genetic lottery having been born with green eyes and red hair, so it's perhaps too much to ask to have also been gifted with the ability to sort my belongings, my to-do list and my life in general into neatly arranged sections. Being organized has to be carried on some gene; it just has to be that way. Perhaps when the scientists are mapping the human genome, one gene will stand out. All the cellular material will be sorted into neat lines. The chromosomes will all be complete and perfectly matched. The cytoplasm won't wobble around all gooey and out of control, and the nucleus will be signaling all the parts one by one in a very orderly fashion to do all the tasks that cells do to make the gene work. This discovery will come across the electron microscope of some PhD and a great "Eureka!" will go up in the lab when at last, the gene for efficiency is found. One thing is for sure though, it won't be found anywhere near my DNA.

I will never be one of those people who puts everything where it goes, whose home is always neat and tidy, and who never misses an appointment or forgets a birthday. There's no excuse for it either. With today's technology, there isn't always a need to go searching for a pen and paper to write things down. There are smartphones with voice notes, reminder apps and calendar programs that can sync schedules between your phone, your laptop and your office email server.

It's like the Six Million Dollar Man; we have the technology. No one is a bigger fan of gadgets and gear than me, but going paperless? No, that just would not happen in my world. My struggles with organization are epic, so it seems the less paperwork there is to deal with, the better off I would be, but it just doesn't work that way. I don't want to give up my chic little Moleskin notebooks and fountain pens. Much like my .38, you can have my stationery when you pry it from my cold dead hand.

So what's the answer? Organization is such a broad concept. It's hard to wrap your head around the entire idea of having a place for everything and everything in its place. The problem for people like me is more complicated. Putting things away neatly and getting rid of clutter seems like it would be easy, but it's not. Well, OK, it's easy for some people, just not for me. To be honest, I harbor more than a slight suspicion that some of the really organized people I know might need medication. I still fail miserably at it though, losing my keys three times a day and tripping over the shoes that are all over the house. What about delegating some of it? There are people for this, experts that come when you call. Throw enough cash at them and the problem is solved.

If your wallet is a little light, then look around at your friends. Don't we all know that one person who is organizationally gifted? Maybe you can do something that friend can't - like bake killer chocolate brownies or knit amazing scarves and hats. Make a deal and do some bartering. A couple of people I know have come to my rescue more than once to keep me from being featured on an episode of "Hoarders." In exchange I have fed them, watched their children, sent them several bottles of the adult beverage of their choice, and on one occasion wrote a resume and cover letter. Everyone has something to offer that someone else wants; we can always find a way to help each other. Networking isn't just for the business world.

To be fair, organization, or the lack of it, isn't just about where your stuff is and how your schedule is arranged. It's about eliminating the stress that happens when your surroundings are a chaotic mix of missing socks, crooked pictures and piles of books and papers. It's much more soothing to look around a room and see couches with soft cushions, shelves neatly arranged and cabinets that don't spew forth an avalanche of appliances and junk when they're opened. Not everyone can do it though. A friend mentioned to me once that she was all freaked out over the organization issue. It was making her nuts that things were out of place, but getting them organized was also stressful. She had read this new book, from author Marie Kondo, *The Life Changing Magic of Tidying Up*. Well, who wouldn't go for a book like that? Life changing? Magic? Sign me up. Apparently if you put your socks in the drawer the right way, they are happy. As we all know, if the socks are happy, everyone is happy. The way you fold things matters. If you want your Lululemons to bring you joy, they need to be stacked correctly. Or something.

This theory suggests that instant, life-changing magic happens when your dresser drawers are properly arranged and your socks are content. So for my friend, in addition to caring about the happiness of her husband and children, she now had to worry about whether or not her clothes were happy. This book had her losing her mind over not only cleaning up, but also keeping her socks comfortable and making sure her jeans were joyful. I tried (and failed) not to laugh in her face.

The book and the method of tidying up it talks about is supposed to make you happy because you've cleaned out a closet or two. Then what? Maybe you've blown off some steam setting the playroom toy bins to rights, sorting out the linen closet or detailing your car.

For the time being, you have tamed the beast. That beast is named Stress though and he will show up again for sure, because while Stress kills, he never dies. It's really a chicken and egg thing. Is the anxiety from the mess, or did the mess happen because we are too wigged out about something else to have kept an eye on the clutter? Either way, the common thread is the mental stress going on. It's everywhere in our lives. It can't be avoided entirely. But if you're losing your mind over organization, and the process of getting organized also makes you crazy, I guarantee your head is going to explode at some point.

The beauty of being the smart, evolved people we are though is that we can choose. We can look at a closet and hyperventilate about the unhappily folded socks and the joyless jeans or we can say to ourselves, "Not today. Today the sun is out, the grass is green and the beach is calling me." We have that power over clutter, and we have it over whatever else is worrying us too. That is what is life changing and magic. Making the choice to leave the clutter where it is and move the stress to the trash barrel. In short, it's not about where you put your things, or at least it shouldn't be. It's about where put you put your mental effort. It's hard to stay afloat when you don't know which way the shore is.

Getting your head in order is the real key to keeping it together and this is where I have the most trouble. For some time now I have alternated between thinking I might have ADHD and being fully convinced that the early onset of dementia has set in. There seems to be no in-between. It's either a minor case of an attentional disorder, or I'm going to die a horrible death but only after lingering for years in a ratty bathrobe asking my kids who they are and why they're in my house. That's because no matter how hard I try to retain information, it seems to leak right out of my head like maple sap on a spring day in Vermont.

I really hope it's not age. You don't start forgetting things when you're still in your 50's right? If 50 is the new 30, doesn't that mean by age 70, I should still be as sharp as I was when I was 40? Here we have math, and that never goes well for me. Shouldn't this mental fog come along much later in life? If I'm going to start losing brain cells now, what if there aren't enough left when it's time to retire? What a cruel joke that would be. Finally it's the part of my life where I can do anything, unencumbered by a job or raising kids, and what happens? I can't keep times and dates straight and instead of traveling the world I just watch the Travel Channel because I have lost the remote.

I think there is no choice but to simply come out of the fog. It will be a fight for sure, but going gentle into that good night of forgetfulness isn't for me. For once, the low-tech way is probably going to be my best bet. My weapon of choice in addition to my precious Moleskin notebooks? Post-It Notes. No kidding: If these sticky little miracles did not exist, I would literally be lost. They are all over my house, and they read like a bad case of Tourette's. "Get drugs, shit in the yard, dirty underwear, hungry, bread, milk, batteries!" Translation: Go to the pharmacy, the yard is full of puppy presents, do the laundry, get groceries and oh yeah, it's going to snow.

It isn't just the daily tasks that get jotted down. Story ideas come when they are least expected, and if they aren't hastily scrawled somewhere that very instant, they vanish. Usually I find paper, but there have been times when a cocktail napkin and eyeliner were all that was available. I can forget a concept from one paragraph to the next, so while I'm tapping away at my laptop, there must be a stack of scrap paper and a Paper-Mate Ink Joy pen right on the desk next to me. Nobody touches my Ink Joy pens if they value their chubby little fingers.

Finally, when you have your head settled and your things put away, you have to figure out where to be and when. The ever-present schedule is something everyone has to deal with. More Post-Its and a dry erase calendar help with this, but I still struggle to remember what day it is every now and then. My family is used to hearing me swear a blue streak when I realize it's Wednesday and not Tuesday. They are also used to acting as a navigator when I'm in the car. My organizational issues extend to getting lost pretty often as well. Much like the rest of staying on top of things, a sense of direction must also be something you are either born with or not. A GPS is a wonderful thing, but I think the disembodied voice that comes out of it on a regular basis is creepy. Especially when it starts bleating, "Re-calculating, re-calculating" when I have gone whizzing by the exit it told me take three times before I got to it.

A good friend has this gift. She is a real fan of maps. Growing up, when her family would take their annual road trip in their Winnebago, she was the map holder. Later on, whenever she was on a plane, she would open her Rand McNally pocket size map book and look out the window to see if she could figure out where she was. To this day, she will draw a diagram complete with roads and landmarks if someone asks for directions. That's why they put her in charge of getting a few hundred troops, several tanks, trucks and an entire mobile air station to Kuwait on 17 hours notice in the first Gulf War. She's a genius.

Once, when visiting her home, I asked how to get to the nearest Starbucks. She said, "Well, you head west out the end of the street, go for about a mile and then head south/southwest along the tree line. It's about 2 miles as the crow flies." Um, hello, do I look like Sacajawea? If there's a tree line and a bird to follow, I'm out. Coffee isn't so important to me that I'd risk having a crow peck at me.

Being organized is certainly helpful, but perhaps not as critical as everyone seems to think. As important as my Post-It notes are to me, they don't make me happy, they just make me do things, and even then, they aren't 100%. On my desk right now is a coffee mug with a broken handle. A friend who is a minister and a potter and puts her whole spirit into her work made it. I dropped it, which surprised no one, because I am unsafe around anything breakable, but I kept it because even something broken can make us happy. It's used for pens and pencils. There's a Murano glass paperweight that's only there because it's my favorite color green. School pictures are paper clipped to the lampshade and there's a little tin box that says "Random Crap" that ironically was a gift from a friend who is a professional organizer. There's a cereal bowl that was hand made by another talented friend. It has never held cereal, but instead a tiny rubber penguin calls it home. I love that little guy.

On the side of a memo board hang two 5K medals, two race bibs, a badminton bird and a Christmas ornament that's a bear. I like bears too; they make me smile. The dresser in my bedroom is much the same: a topsy-turvy, disorganized and cluttered collection of stuff that makes me happy.

We can choose to stress over organization (or whatever the real issue is that's bugging us) or we can choose to look at these haphazard parts of our lives: the job stress, the relationships, and the anxiety and say, "Things can't be all that bad. I have a tiny rubber penguin in a cereal bowl. Maybe I'll put him in my pocket today." The deep end is full of to-do lists, unmet expectations and lost car keys. At some point you have to drop most of that stuff or you might sink. Don't sink; swim. If nothing else, it makes your butt look good.

2

"The only real stumbling block is fear of failure. In cooking you've got to have a what-the-hell attitude."

— Julia Child

If having a "What the hell attitude" was the key to cooking, I'd be the darling of the Food Network. There would be a line of pans with my endorsement, best-selling cookbooks and eventually a lawsuit over something that may or may not have been said by me at my chain of celebrity restaurants. Attitude has never been in short supply in anything I set out to do. That has its good and bad parts, as you can imagine, but it's true. Attitude is everything, right? Even on the days when my attitude has me looking at everyone's head as if it were an invitation to batting practice, it usually serves me well.

It isn't that cooking scares me. It doesn't. Someone told me once that anyone who can read a recipe can cook. You can open up a cookbook (or in these high-tech times, launch a website on your iPad) find something that looks good and just follow the steps. It should be simple, really. There's so much information out there on how to do things. YouTube isn't just a website, it's become a verb, like "Google it!" If a recipe says to debone a chicken, there's a video for that. YouTube it! There are step-by-step tutorials on how to blanch vegetables, make a roux and clarify butter. Butter has never seemed ambiguous to me, but hey, everything turns out better when we're all clear on what exactly is happening. Cook a meal? Sure, even one I've never made before doesn't faze me. I have no natural ability to craft original dishes and create something that has some culinary chutzpah but I can put things in a pan one after the other and wind up with something edible.

Technique is one thing, having a gift for knowing which flavors and ingredients go together well and the creativity to think of new combinations is something else entirely. Whenever there's an item on a menu that reads, "Sea scallops on a bed of mushroom risotto with raspberry-mocha glaze and blue-cheese crumbles with fennel" I wonder who possibly could have come up with the idea to put all those flavors in one dish. Then I put that recipe away because that's just not happening. It was probably the same kind of person who first looked at a cow and said, "You know, there's no reason people can't drink what's leaking out of that big bag; there's plenty to go around."

There is your WTH attitude. That guy (and let's face it, it had to have been a man) was definitely a genius of some kind. A lonely and bored one, most likely, and certainly single, that much has to be true. There he was, stuck out in the barn and probably really thirsty. Perhaps it didn't go well the first few times, but WTH? Whoever it was made it work and we have him to thank for things like chocolate milk and a dipping pool for Oreos.

Going to the store to buy stuff for dinner is no problem either. I love the grocery store; it's like theater for me. It's entirely entertaining now that my kids are out of the meltdown stage to look at some kid torturing herself and everyone around her with a fit over Cap'n Crunch and think, "That Dad is hitting the liquor store on his way home, for sure." Lists are my life, they just work for me, so it's like a scavenger hunt going through the store and getting all the stuff a recipe calls for and then checking it off the list.

Once the food is purchased and brought home, it's fun to spread it all out and line up what needs to go into this new dish. It's a bonus if there was some implement that also had to be bought since I love me some new kitchen gadgets, and the more obscure the better.

Did you know they make a specific tool just for yanking the green tops off strawberries? They do, and there's one in my kitchen drawer. I also have a pepper corer that is specifically for bell peppers, as opposed to the stick thingy that is for chili peppers. That famous routine with Ralph Kramden and Ed Norton selling the multitasking gadget for the "Chef of the Future" is not for me. I own at least a dozen tools that can do one thing and one thing only. Next time you're shopping, check out the kitchen gear section; it's amazing the things they have.

So now the food has been procured, it's in the kitchen, and the cookbook is at the ready. I've donned my "Will Cook for Shoes" pink apron, poured a tiny glass of wine a la Julia, and I'm wielding a rubber spatula that says "Naughty" on it. It was part of a set I wound up with at a Yankee Swap. The other one said "Nice" but a WTH attitude in the kitchen calls for some naughty. It's "go time."

But wait... what are we making? That, ladies and gentlemen, is where you lose me. In my house we have a free-speech policy, at least partially. Adults are the only ones allowed to use certain words. Respect and kindness are goals, if not always a reality, but otherwise you can say whatever you want. However, the children have been warned not to ask me, "What's for dinner?" It will not end well. There is no phrase I hate hearing more, with the possible exception of "I found a bug in my hair." For the love of all that is holy and good on this earth, please do not make me decide what to have; it's truly a bridge too far for me these days. Who knows why this final step eludes me, but it does.

The problem is this: when one of the children asks what's for dinner, usually my answer is a list of a few very basic meals that are always easy to whip up. Spaghetti and meatballs. Chicken pie. Homemade butternut squash soup and grilled Monte Cristo sandwiches with ham and cheese. Noodles with broccoli and cheese. Bacon and eggs. Pancake night. But no, that's never good enough. Those choices are met with a chorus of, "Ugh! I don't like tacos." "Why can't we have ramen noodles?" "Can I just have cereal?"

This is when my voice takes on that hard edge that signals I'm about spew something. More than once I have interrupted their whining by whistling through my fingers and bellowing, "Listen up kiddos. You don't like those choices? Then don't ask me what's for dinner! Get your over-entitled little arses into the kitchen and figure it out!" These moments are not the finest examples of my patience and parenting, but so far no one has starved to death.

I'm really just trying to get them to meet me halfway. Every time the shopping list is being prepared, requests are always solicited. If they want something else, they can ask for it, like people who have the power of speech do. They could text me if they wanted to, and then I could add the items to my handy-dandy iPhone shopping list app, but unless they tell me what they would like, it's just not going to happen.

My children spend a fair amount of time on the Internet. How about downloading a few chicken recipes there, Devin? Think outside the box of rice pilaf, George. Everything to do with feeding our family is done by me, and it's a pleasure, really. It would just be nice to have them think for themselves a little and come up with some ideas. Perhaps this is my version of that WTH attitude. My darlings, if you don't like what's here then be the change you wish to see at the dinner table. They're tired of the usual, and that's fine, but I'm tired of biting my tongue and not answering that forbidden question with, "How the hell should I know?" It shouldn't be this difficult. It's a constant struggle to get the little buggers to work with me. Perhaps eventually they will get awfully sick of Taco Tuesdays and Cheap Chicken Thursdays, but until then, the food I buy is all that's on the menu.

That covers how the food gets made, but to back it up a little, doesn't the attitude toward food start with how we think about it? James Beard said, *"Good bread is the most fundamentally satisfying of all foods; good bread with fresh butter, the greatest of feasts!"* and I think what he must have meant is that food should be simple. It should be fresh and satisfying, rather than over-thought and overwrought, right? Does it have to be such a big deal?

Fresh bread right out of the oven is irresistible to me. It's practically impossible for me to get home from the store with a whole loaf of fresh-baked Italian bread. That loaf will be long gone by the time I pull into my driveway. Crusty outside, warm and doughy inside and that yummy smell? If there are people that can resist that, well, they have more willpower than most. It's the most basic food item on your average shopping list, but when it's done right, good bread and a little butter is heavenly.

When it comes to what we eat, simple is always best. I don't know what's happened to food lately, but it's become way more complicated than it needs to be. We've got enough to do without worrying about every last detail of what's on the plate. Growing up, our house was strictly meat and potatoes — heavy on the potatoes, being as Irish as we were. It wasn't about flavor blends and a mingling of spices. It was about putting food on the table that looked like the magazine ads of the time. Balanced meals were perfectly proportioned on a nice plate, full of all-American comfort food. It wasn't about gourmet gastronomy or haute cuisine. It was just food.

Those divided trays you see in cafeterias could have been the road map for the food that landed on our table. One section of meat, one of potatoes, one of something green. Everything on the plate was cooked until it was beyond recognition. It was just that simple. Looking back, yes, it wasn't very appetizing and probably not all that healthy, since the vegetables always came out of a can full of salty water and the meat was likely full of chemicals. The basics of those bygone days have been replaced with so much more. Creativity is good to have in the kitchen, but are we overthinking food now?

Produce is best when it's bought fresh, that's a given. But now there are codes on all the fruit and vegetables. Some have four digits and some have five. And those aren't so the store knows to ring up the right price. Those numbers tell you if the produce is organic or genetically modified. I did a little research on the whole genetically modified food issue, and I'd like to say that now I fully understand the concept. Except I don't and I'm not sure anyone does. If the code on that avocado you want to buy begins with an "8," it's genetically modified; if it begins with a "9," it's organic. If there is no "8" or "9," it's "nonqualified" or conventionally grown — which could mean just about anything. Is there a way to unconventionally grow an avocado? Perhaps if you wear a ball gown and water the tree with a squirt gun that's unconventional, but they don't have a code for that.

Even the term "genetically modified" is pretty scary. Is there a lab somewhere with carrot DNA being blended in a petri dish with cabbage DNA to make some kind of cloned coleslaw?

And it's really no different in a restaurant. Menus have whole paragraphs describing the entrees. "Wild-caught Chilean sea bass, on a bed of organic Brussels sprouts marinated in extra virgin olive oil and non-alcoholic red wine vinegar. Grilled over a fire of responsibly harvested hard wood from reclaimed forest land managed by the indigenous population of a democratically governed country." OK, maybe it doesn't say all that, but sometimes I know more about my food than I do about the person with whom I'm having dinner. Wild-caught sea bass as opposed to what? The sea bass that turned itself in? "Extra virgin olive oil?" It's not even good enough anymore to be a regular virgin, there's an extra something required? I can't imagine what that would be.

It just seems that putting the life story of a fish on the menu is overkill, but restaurants now will tell you almost anything you want to know about your meal. The rest your waiter will fill you in on, like if the lobster you ordered had any hobbies. What happened to just getting a burger and fries? Or fish and chips? Those basic dishes can be served and enjoyed without having to publish a dissertation on wildlife conservation. Breakfast can just be corn flakes or a scrambled egg and toast; you don't have to have a bowl full of organic nuts and grains, immersed in soy milk and sprinkled with sweetener made from crushed plant leaves. A ham and cheese sandwich on plain old white bread can be packed for lunch, with a thermos of lukewarm milk and a couple of Oreo cookies, and I promise you, the food police will not come after you. Every once in a while, go "old school" and have something dangerous. It isn't news that Pop Tarts aren't the best nutrition. We don't need the FDA telling us that bacon isn't heart healthy. But bacon is awesome, and Pop Tarts are fun.

"Keep it simple" is a good way to think about food. What was always good is still good. Crunchy vegetables. Warm cookies. Almost anything with cheese melted on it. There doesn't have to be an encyclopedia of information on every bite of food. Not every meal has to have twenty-seven specific ingredients, and spices and sauces that bring out the complex flavor tones. A fresh loaf of bread, some good cheese, a few slices of ham and some salty olives is an amazingly simple and delicious snack that doesn't require any talent in the kitchen — which makes it a frequent staple in my house because while I definitely have the attitude, I don't really have the talent to go with it. I also don't have the patience to assemble anything requiring more than three or four items and a can of cream-of-chicken soup.

Food should be fun. It can be something we celebrate with and something that brings us together, it should also be part of our childhood memories. Comfort food is called that for a reason. What it doesn't have to be is complicated. Does it really have to be all about what's on your table? Can't it be about who is at your table? A good friend was telling me about his grandfather and how close they were. He would stop by his granddad's house about once a week with a meal he had cooked, and spend some time. I asked him what he made and what the favorites were but he couldn't really say exactly. It was just food. I'll have what he's having.

3

"There is nothing on this earth more to be prized than friendship."

----*Thomas Aquinas*

To have friends is the greatest gift we can be given. While there are a dozen cheesy quotes and phrases about friendship, it's really quite simple: friends are the pieces of our souls that walk around outside of ourselves. There should never be a day that doesn't involve a good friend, even for a moment. They are the reason for that quick text or email you shoot out when something funny happens. A cup of coffee to catch up, a drink after work, or a phone call to pass the time when you're stuck in traffic are all small bits of friendship that keep us anchored when the winds might otherwise carry us out to sea.

I have been beyond lucky when it comes to friends. Whether it's geographically, philosophically or just in numbers, there isn't anywhere I could go, or anything that could happen to me that I could not share with a good friend, or five. Not that it's a contest, because the thing about friendship is that quality trumps quantity every time. It's just that the right person, if it's a good friend, can conquer the world with you. One good friend can be the designated driver for a much needed girls night out, or pick up your kid from school when you can't. One good friend can sit across the table from you while you cry about something stupid and know, instinctively, whether to just hold your hand or tell you it's stupid and to snap out of it.

Good friends keep us whole, sometimes literally. There is this one person I know and she's a nurse, a dancer, a wife and a mother but most importantly she is my friend. There are countless stories of gut-busting funny adventures that we've been on with each other. We've been tossed out of bars together, we've cried and laughed, (usually at the same time) and it's all been this very long, strange trip that I hope never ends. Lucy and Ethel, Betty and Wilma and even Thelma and Louise have nothing on Rosemary and me.

We have paraded down Royal St. in the French Quarter of New Orleans while tossing beads at tourists, and we've faced Black Friday armed with nothing but a MasterCard and good running shoes. We had sworn an oath, and as God as our witness, that Lego Star Wars Millennium Falcon was going under the tree that Christmas. When you have a little boy that needs to believe Santa can do anything, a good friend will be there in the trenches, lining up at the crack of Jesus, just because you ask her to.

We've rafted down Class V rapids in Colorado and rode horses through the Rocky Mountains praying we got back in one piece. This one summer, we drove all over Hell's Half Acre going to diners and asking for recipes because we were going to write a diner cookbook--until we walked into a diner that had three different ones for sale. It was worth it though, we had some mighty good pie…and BBQ…and macaroni and cheese, but so what? That fall, the gym had a two-for-one special, so it was a win after all. That's another thing good friends do, they jump in on any idea you have and the only questions they might ask are "Who's driving?" or "Is this a one bottle of wine thing, or should I break out the vodka and cigarettes?"

That's not to say that friendship is all fun and games. It most certainly isn't. Sometimes it sucks, but it's during those times that you figure out who is with you, and who can be jettisoned over the side of the S.S. Friendship without a backward glance. There are also times when it's uneven. Asking for help can be hard, no matter how close you are to someone. Scary things like divorce, cancer and addiction will test the bounds of any friendship. The Beatles were right to use the plural when they sang, "I get by with a little help from my friends..." There are times when there is only one person you can share something with and then there are times when you need to call in the entire crew.

The Irish Women's Committee is my go-to for any issue that requires more than a cup of tea or a shot of tequila. It's a group that started when we were young (and not so young) mothers and part of the same church playgroup. We'd meet once a week in the parish hall and there would be some toys, some coffee and for an hour or so we were dressed and out of the house which, when you have small children, is sometimes the only win you're going to get on any given day. As it happened, we all grew up in similar families and shared the experience of being the children of Irish parents. Stories of fathers who told tall tales and mothers who screamed out the window "Jesus Mary and Joseph, get your arse in here..." were exchanged and a bond was formed. Those little kids who toddled around on the floor playing are all grown up now, for the most part, but the Irish Women's Committee remains. It's not really a formal thing, but we all know if one of us is in trouble, we are all in trouble together.

When I encountered a series of lucky and unlucky events that eventually unfolded into being diagnosed with ovarian cancer, it suddenly became a problem no amount of wine and laughter could solve. Who did I call? Well, OK, I pretty much called everyone I knew, freaking out in a most spectacular fashion and venting all over anyone who picked up the phone. While there were dozens of people that made meals for me, picked up kids, and sent funny cards and books, it was Rosemary and the IWC that kept me afloat in the deep end during that time. It was a case of the sum of the parts being greater than the whole. Yes, that isn't mathematically possible, but math is not relevant in these situations.

It started with Rosemary. She's an oncology nurse and if you have cancer, she is who you want on your side. People say that we seek in others that which we do not find in ourselves. While I am often loud, rude, profane and opinionated, she is quiet, polite, diplomatic and smart. An ER doctor found my tumor quite by accident, and while it went well enough at that point, going forward into more surgery and treatment was a task for specialists. Living in the Northeast is a bonus because this is where the best hospitals and doctors in the world are. A drive along my beloved ocean would put me in the center of the best care available on the planet.

In any crisis, there is that first moment of shock and fear that holds us frozen like a deer in the headlights before we figure out what to do. It truly is that moment where we must sink or swim. Lucky for me, I had help. Rosemary went into her office the next day and proceeded to open up a can of medical whoop ass, in her very polite and diplomatic way. Her office is chock full of cancer nurses (true heroes, every last one of them), doctors, and resources from the best hospital in the world. She knew exactly the doctor I needed to see and what the course of treatment would be and she wasn't going to stop until there was an appointment made. Here's something most people don't realize. When someone is on a mission to help a friend, they will be ruthless. Friends will kick down doors, they will break bones, and some will break laws if necessary, but the person who rides hard and fast to the rescue, no matter what? That's the person you want in your corner.

I was seen the next day, thanks to her efforts, and in the months that followed, she continued to be there, as did the Irish Women. It's not just the meals and the errands that are important, although they were much appreciated. It's the quiet presence of a force that you know is there, just under the surface of the deep end, ready to be summoned, sometimes even before you know you need it.

Women, at least the ones I know, have some kind of ESP (Estrogen Super Power) that kicks in when one of the tribe is in need.

There is no explanation other than good karma for how my friend Catherine knew to come to the door the very day my pathology results came back. Catherine is a founding member of the Irish Women's Committee and someone who has seen the deep end of too many places. Her gift is that she knows the way back. She was sitting across the kitchen table from me when the phone rang and she knew, as did I, that this was "the call." I don't remember exactly what the doctor said, or what I said until I heard "the margins are clear, we got it all." Poor Catherine could only see my white knuckled hand gripping the phone and could only hear me say, "OK. Yes. Thank you." but for her, it didn't matter. She had come because I needed her and she would do whatever it took to help, good news or bad. Fortunately the news was good, and having her be the one to hear it first was just more proof that some things are meant to happen, rather than accidents of fate or coincidence.

People think that when bad things happen, this is when you send up a flare and gather your crew and while that's true, it's not all there is to friendship. When you find yourself back on shore after a long time in rough water, this is the best time to put out the call for a different reason. The Great St. Patrick's Day Do-Over of 2013 was just such an occasion. The friends who had kept my head above water deserved a party in their honor, as a thank you for every card, every meal and every time they listened to me whine, worry and weep. I had missed St. Patrick's Day in the midst of all the cancer shenanigans, but I am Irish all the time, not just in March. On a hot June night, the rafters rang with wine and song. Toasts, tears and at least a few choruses of

"Whiskey You're the Devil" made it a night to remember, even if some of it is a bit of blur for me.

In good times and in bad, the company you keep matters. The same friends that would skip beside me with a baseball bat singing "someone's gonna get it" if I asked them to would also tell me to the put the bat away and get the hell over myself if that's what I needed. Women especially have a hard time asking for help, but we are usually the first to offer it. Why is that? Why can't we say to someone else "I need help" when the tide is high and we need a lifeline? My friends have been there for me hundreds of times, and I wouldn't hesitate to be there for any of them either. When it comes right down to it, no one has ever gotten out of a tough spot alone. Perhaps it isn't obvious on the surface, but anyone who has been through something really bad has had at least a bit of help, even if it was just the memory of something a friend said or did that they clung to when it was dark. Friendship is a gift, but it doesn't do you any good if you never open it. If you're lucky enough to have friends, you are lucky enough.

4

"The price of anything is the amount of life you exchange for it."

---Ralph Waldo Emerson

Money can be a taboo topic, but it shouldn't be. Almost everyone has some kind of budget. No one has an unlimited supply of cash, at least no one I can think of. If there are people who can spend whatever they want, with no thought to the cost, I haven't come across them during any of my shopping trips. In my house, I do most of the shopping and for me it's definitely a game of making sure there isn't too much month left at the end of the money.

When I am shopping for items like clothes, school supplies or sports gear I look upon that kind of shopping like some people look at golf; I aim low. For ballet class, my daughter needed black leotards. Only black. She wasn't awfully picky then about the style, so I checked the dance boutiques, the malls and websites for the best price. When the specifics don't matter that much, it comes down to how much I want to spend and since I could pretty much squeeze a dime until Roosevelt screams, this is a job that I'm well suited for. The problem can be that the time spent scouring every last resource for the best price cancels out any amount I might save. It is one of the few areas in which I possess a laser-like focus though; it's not over until every option has been tried at least twice.

Big-ticket items like cars or vacations are another area that gets researched to death before the checkbook comes out. There is no rhyme or reason to car prices. You just basically have to know going in what you want and how much you are willing to pay. If you stick to your guns, don't fall for any BS about "dealer prep" charges and are prepared to get up and walk right out of the dealership at any point, I guarantee you will come out ahead. When I walked out of the salesman's office during the negotiating process on the last car I bought, there was a call from him the next day meeting my price. In business though time is money; another $100 was deducted from my bottom line because it took a day. If there is a card dealer's hit list, it's a safe bet my name appears on it.

Hotel rooms and plane tickets are even more difficult to nail down. The same exact rooms right next to each other at a hotel could vary in price by hundreds of dollars. Airfares are notoriously complex; the airlines can't even tell you why one seat is more than another on the same flight. Spending a little time checking around pays off, and I like the thrill of the chase.

Therein lies the catch with shopping. It costs money. Money matters but the topic is prickly and uncomfortable. While it might seem basic in that each of us has a certain amount of money coming in and a certain amount of expenses and debts that have to be paid, it's not exactly that simple. If there is a little left over after you pay what you owe, then there's some wiggle room but no one can seem to agree on what is worth spending money on and what isn't. This leftover money is often referred to as "disposable income" but never by me. None of my income is disposable. Paper cups might be, but money is not. It's more like discretionary spending and it's different for everyone. We all decide what's worth splurging on and what isn't and as long as no one is starving, buying a little something now and then is retail therapy and it works. There's a line though, in talking about money and discussing how much we have or don't have, and it's hard to know where it is, until you've crossed over it.

It's especially difficult with our kids. How much should we tell our kids about money? Should they have their own money? When and how much of an allowance should they get? Can they spend their allowance on anything they want? These are the tough questions that face parents on the money issue and it almost becomes like negotiating a car purchase, except no one gets to walk out.

I got an allowance growing up, and it was the first time I remember even thinking about money. When I was about 8, a candy bar was a dime. My father decided I could have an allowance of a dollar a week. Given my remedial math skills, it took me until the end the first week to figure out that I could buy a candy bar every day of the week and still have money left over. I don't think I have ever felt richer.

When I was older and babysitting, the going rate was a dollar an hour. That is a lot of candy bars. Babysitting twice a week, I could earn 10 bucks, and for me that was like having all the money in the world. I was 15, I didn't have to pay bills, and I didn't have to buy my own clothes and food, so most of the time I blew all that money on movies and Bonne Bell Lip Smackers. There was, however, one summer when I saved every penny I made to buy a boom box. It was the size of a microwave oven and took 16 D-cell batteries, but it was all mine.

Prices have changed a lot since then, but it's really the same dilemma for parents. Not only is the allowance question tricky, but kids will ask about family income as well. How much does daddy make? How much did our house cost? I was going through files and found the tax return from the year I had my first child. The deduction was nice, but I can't believe

I forgot how little we made as a family that year. When I remember how much baby things cost and the fact that I had taken half the year off from work, I think we must have eaten a lot of pasta and hot dogs for supper.

I know my parents did the same thing. One night, during the first year of their marriage, my mother was pregnant and my father was working two jobs and bartending on the side. No matter how they shuffled the envelopes of cash and the monthly bills on the kitchen table, the numbers were not adding up. My father tossed down his pencil and said, "I've had enough of this" and stormed out of the house. He returned about an hour later with two really good steaks and a bouquet of flowers. He cooked the steak while my mother lost her mind shrieking about the rent and the bills and when she stopped he said, "Babe, we can't make the bills this month, so a few people will have to wait. In the meantime, if I'm on my way to bankruptcy and financial ruin, we might as well make it a night to remember." He picked up a few extra bartending jobs the next week, the phone company didn't shut them off and it all worked out. Money matters, but it shouldn't be something that takes over our lives.

Years later things were very different for my parents. My father had given up odd jobs and bartending and had opened his own company and eventually he did really well. I remember asking him once if we were rich because he was the boss now. He said "Rich? Not anymore. I just sunk our life savings into buying a company; it's baloney sandwiches for a little while." I know now that it took two years before the business showed a profit, and it was a huge risk that fortunately paid off for our family. I learned from my father's attitude about money that it wasn't how much you made, but how much you were willing to do.

When my oldest was about 5, I was working as a waitress in a diner. Not a high-paying job and I certainly wasn't knocking them dead in the corporate world, but still, it was a good fit for us at the time. I would come home with my apron pockets jingling with change that needed counting. And my son and I would sit at the table and line up all the dimes, nickels, quarters and pennies and then put them in wrappers. It was just a game at the time, but looking back, it's a very concrete way to teach a child about money. I was gone, I came back, I had money. For a 5-year-old, that really was enough for him to know. That's how the world works: If you want money, you go earn it. I didn't have this job when my other two children were little, and that is probably why they think money comes from the magic ATM.

My children have an allowance like I did, but a larger amount because of inflation. They get one dollar per grade year. I think I read somewhere once that it was a good system for most kids, so that is what they get. According to them, they are the lowest-paid children on the planet, but I am holding firm. When George pointed out that his friend "Sam" got $6 a week to his $2 a week, I explained that Sam's mom required him to save $2 for college and put $2 in the collection basket at church. I told him I was perfectly willing to renegotiate his compensation package and that I was sure that Father Burns would be thrilled to see him contributing every week at Mass. Also, all that extra money in his college fund 10 years down the road would definitely help me out too. He shut up pretty quick about Sam and his fortune after that discussion.

I think it's a learning experience for them to make their own decisions on how to spend their money, with some limits of course. My daughter wanted to buy a hamster once, with her savings. A hamster is nothing but a rat with good hair, and I am not having that in my house. She did however save up enough to buy an enormous stuffed panda bear. The thing is huge, and every time I come around the corner to her room it scares the hell out of me. But it took 10 weeks of not spending a penny so she could get it, and that is an accomplishment.

Money and all that goes along with making it, spending it and saving it can be a sticky subject, but it can't be ignored. Kids aren't born knowing about money; they start out thinking the money just appears, because for some kids it kind of does. In some towns there are 16-year-olds driving cars that cost more than some of their teachers make in a year. But that same 16-year-old is going to have to pay rent some day and buy food and clothes. The last thing we want for our children is to have them drowning in the deep end of debt. Teaching a kid to drive is nice, but showing them how to get somewhere is more important.

Where do you begin though, in this financial education? You could start with coupons. If coffee is $8.00 a pound can they afford it? Maybe a coupon would make it easier to buy the things they want? Just make sure they don't turn into an extreme coupon collector. Yes, that's right, there is an extreme version of glancing at ads and getting a few deals.

Apparently there are people who take coupons pretty seriously. On some reality show I caught once while channel surfing, there was a woman in a recycling dumpster with her four year-old digging for extra fliers to get more coupons. Not exactly the way most kids want to learn how to spend their allowances. I know families have to find ways to cut back, but if the day comes when I'm rummaging through dumpsters for a buy-one get-one free coupon for Chips Ahoy cookies, well that is the day I hope a bus hits me on the way home.

These shoppers dedicate huge chunks of time to this process. Trips to the store can take six or seven hours, and fill a dozen carts. Sometimes they need two cars to get everything home. I like shopping, in the sense that it's about having a list, getting in and getting out. I like seeing how fast I can find everything. Not for nothing, if I had to spend six hours in a grocery store, I would not live long enough to enjoy the eighty-seven jars of chunk pineapple I got for a buck. The stress, the music and mostly the other shoppers would cause a vein in my head to explode about three hours in, leaving me twitching on the floor surrounded by double coupons and cases of Ramen Noodles. After they've loaded up the loot, these edgy, twitchy, paper-snatching super shoppers have to go home and put it all way in their ruthlessly organized stockpiles. It just doesn't seem like something kids would want to do.

What about garage sales? I have always been a fan of garage sales. Even before the Home and Garden Network made them trendy, I was following signs nailed to telephone poles in a modern-day treasure hunt. I will buy just about anything if I think it's a bargain. Maybe having a family yard sale and letting the kids run it would be a good idea to show them how much something is worth?

That's what we did when all the toys and games had reached critical mass in my house. It was the first and last garage sale we will ever do. I found that I enjoyed going to them way more than I enjoyed having one. There was too much stuff that we didn't use though and we needed the room to buy more stuff that we would use. I really think that's what yard sales are all about. Everyone just trades the junk they have for the junk someone else has. The same mermaid statue with a clock in the tail is likely making its way around the world, one garage sale at a time.

The kids did pretty well with their end of the sale, having realized that the toys they no longer wanted were new to someone else. There was one tough moment when my daughter had second thoughts about selling a doll that she'd had forever. She got all *Toy Story* on me thinking that her Emma doll would miss her. I reminded her that we had picked up Emma doll at a yard sale and it was time for someone else to have a turn. Also, Emma doll fetched $3 and that's how much it was for the hair chalk she wanted. Sold!

Finally, no matter what the money situation is, everyone likes a treat now and then. I instituted "Treat Day" with my kids when I got tired of them asking to stop at the convenience store every day after school. On Friday, if the week had gone well, we could go and they could pick out a normally forbidden soda, candy bar or even a bag of some fatty disgusting chips. Once a week, no more than that. They were not entitled to Treat Day; it was done only if their behavior warranted it. Once in a great while, it was upgraded to a trip to a store that had toys or other fun stuff, and they could spend up to $5. Money doesn't have to be a stressful thing. Sometimes it can just be about a candy bar and a yard sale doll. Keeping it simple and straightforward is best, because it's really easy to sink where money is involved. Couples fight about money more than any other issue, so making sure our kids don't look at it like it's something to be feared is giving them an advantage no amount of cash can buy.

5

"Wisdom doesn't necessarily come with age. Sometimes age just shows up all by itself."

— *Tom Wilson*

Age shows up on everyone if they are lucky. The alternative to getting older is not something I would choose. No thank you, there are much better options. So we put up with the inconvenience of reading glasses. Perhaps we are slower on the daily run. Maybe we walk now, instead of running. The memory goes a little and walking into a room and forgetting why you went there in the first place is the new normal. Grey hair is a reality.

OK, well in the interest of full disclosure, that is one area where I will yield no ground. Yes, I'm a red head. I was born one, and I will die one. What happens in the meantime is a magical combination of a brilliant hairdresser and my own stubborn refusal to go gentle into that snow-capped winter. If we are talking seasons, I would like to stay firmly in autumn, with red gold leaves and bright crisp days.

There seems to be no standard anymore on what is old, though, and I for one think that's a good thing. There are teachers at the high school my children attend that were there when I graduated back in the 80's. They seemed old then. Now? Not so much. The media has moved the line ahead several years on what constitutes being old and unlike most of what the media tells us, I believe this. I look at someone who is 50 and think, "You're not old; you're just getting started."

I like to practice what I preach so when I reached that milestone of 50 years, instead of grabbing a bottle of Jameson and hiding under my bed in a deep hormonal psychosis, mourning my lost youth, I decided a really great party would be a much better idea. Also, we were out of Jameson.

Nothing keeps you feeling young like planning a party. And it's totally not true that throwing a party for yourself is a breach of etiquette. Sometimes, when you're getting close to the deep end, a party is just what you need, and if no one else is stepping up, there is no shame in taking matters into your own hands and doing it yourself. Isn't that the way to make sure it's done right? I was lucky enough to have a friend who was also turning 50 so it was a party for both of us. She didn't actually turn 50 until a few days after the party though, she's a just a tad younger than I am, but who's counting? Well, she was and as a matter of fact insisted that it be made clear to all who attended that she wasn't 50 just yet. It's OK, age is supposed to be all your head anyway right? In my head I'm still 25 so it all works out.

"A Night in 1964" is what we called it. If you're going to have a party, you should have a really good theme. Every year has historical events and happenings, but 1964 was quite something. The Ford Mustang rolled off the assembly line, the Beatles took America by storm and Apollo 1, the beginning of the effort to send a man to the moon, was launched. Time travel isn't possible but on this night, it was 1964. We had a photo booth because while selfies are what people do today at parties, in 1964, they climbed into photo booths and made silly faces. The photo booth is the original selfie.

SINK OR SWIM: TALES FROM THE DEEP END OF EVERYWHERE

The appetizers were from my mother's 1960s edition of the Better Homes and Gardens Cookbook. The music included the Fab Four, Sinatra, the Supremes and lots of other 60's hits. "Mad Men" and all that was chic and swingy in 1964 made turning 50 a lot more fun than it might have otherwise been.

Once the party has been cleaned up though, we still have to get through the rest of being a "certain age." It's not all bad though. Once you turn 50, you can become a member of the American Association of Retired Persons. There's no way I will be able to retire at 50, but the discounts they offer on hotels and movie passes are pretty good. Many restaurants offer senior-citizen dinner specials. Of course, they are usually at 4:30 p.m., but still, it's something to think about, right? OK, well, maybe that AARP card is a bit of a buzz kill, but turning 50, or 65 or 80 shouldn't be something negative. Maybe it's not the most fun you've ever had, especially when you consider the embarrassing and invasive medical tests that now have to be endured (you never see a colonoscopy party invite do you?) but no matter what, a number shouldn't ever determine who you are or what you are capable of, whether it's your age, your salary or your dress size.

Then there is the wisdom thing. Aren't we supposed to get smarter as we get older? Haven't we seen more and done more than our younger counterparts? Well, not always. Technology has allowed someone who is 20 to have experienced things someone who is 60 never could have imagined. Just because someone in my age group has dialed a rotary phone and covered a textbook with a grocery bag doesn't automatically make us wiser. Sometimes age is just that, a bunch of years that have gone by. The years should bring wisdom, that's what everyone says, but it doesn't always work that way. Some people didn't get their share, for whatever reason, and they might have the years but not the knowledge.

There are wise young people and a few stupid old people, but I was fortunate enough to know Mary Quinn, a fine Irish woman, who had seen more and knew more than almost everyone and yet at the same time was younger than springtime. She lived her life minding her own business. She always said, "Mind your own business, because if you're minding your own business you've no time to mind anyone else's." She believed that when we meddled in other people's lives instead of taking care of what was in our own lives, that trouble would surely follow. She was right.

She was equally at ease in someone's kitchen helping with the dishes, on the deck of a country club, or in the yard with her grandchildren. We should all hope to get to the age she got to and to have learned as much as she did along the way. She was a woman who had to work harder to stay afloat than anyone should have to, and what she learned from that was that no matter where you were on the number line, it wasn't about the years you had behind you, but rather what was to come.

Why is it that age is seen as a hindrance sometimes? There is a lot of talk in the workplace of mentoring. Someone more experienced in their field will take a less experienced person under their wing and help them along on a career path. I wonder why we don't do that outside of the workplace? Why is it that sometimes the older folks get shuffled to the edges as if they no longer have anything to offer? We may not realize it, but they are a treasure trove of history and experience that cannot be duplicated anywhere.

The History Channel has hundreds of hours of programming on what it was like during World War II. There were women in factories that had never picked up a hammer or a wrench, but they built the planes that won the war. Certain foods were rationed, and there were air-raid drills in schools. They have shows about the first astronauts in the Mercury program where a manned spacecraft orbited the earth for the first time, long before the Apollo moon landings. It's truly fascinating, but there are probably people in our lives who could tell you all about it. Because they lived it. Why don't we take advantage of the wisdom that is sometimes right here among us?

I was at the gym once and as I was hobbling down the stairs after a particularly tough go at the treadmill and elliptical there were a few ladies leaving one of the studios. They looked to be in their late 60's or so. Whether that makes them old, elderly, senior citizens or whatever other term there is for it doesn't matter. Every one of them was looking fabulous, chatting and laughing together and they were handling the stairs better than my sorry butt was. There was a sign outside the studio that said something about a guest speaker and the topic was "End of Life Issues." Seriously, it said that. What kind of aging hell went on in there?

Who wants to go to something like that? Who wants to think about the end of life? This was a gym, isn't that where we go to stay healthy and prolong our lives? I barely restrained myself from running up to them and saying, "What's all that about? None of you are at the end, look at yourselves, you're awesome!"

They'd probably have thought I was some kind of whack job though, and they certainly would not have been alone in that theory. Perhaps they were there for family members that might be nearing the end, though I hope not. It was likely an advice session on how to set up a will, how to let your family members know what you would like and all that, and it makes sense to have those plans in place, but couldn't it be called something better? I can't imagine anyone going around thinking "I might die soon, better go take a class on that!" Who wants to think about "end of life" issues?

Off the top of my head I can think of a dozen friends of mine in their late 70s, 80s and even a couple that have cracked 90. Not a one of them is anywhere near the end of anything but the latest bestseller and the last season of Downton Abbey. Yes, we can all do the math; no one lives to be 165, so my dear friend Annie who just celebrated a birthday that begins with an 8 isn't middle aged, I get that. It's not near the end for her though and it's not even close to the end for Cheri, Jean, Mary, Nan, Anita, Bob, Gino, Colonel Woody or any of my other more "senior" friends. It's just not.

Planning things like wills, trusts and finances is just business. It's a little paperwork you do to help out the ones left behind. My plans are made, that box is checked off, so I'm calling it done and getting busy planning career moves, trips and time with friends and family. If you haven't seen to this kind of thing, you should, and that goes for anyone over the age of 18. Then, once you're done, forget about the end of your life and get on with the rest of your life. The best is yet to come.

Wisdom doesn't come only with age. It also comes from paying attention to what goes on around you. It comes from being present in the moments that matter. In that sense, we could all be wise regardless of our age. But because it doesn't always work that way maybe we could ask someone older than ourselves, someone from another generation, a few things they think are important to know. A wiser and much older person told me once that it's a poor day when you don't learn something new. It's also a good idea to learn something old once in a while, too, I think.

6

"The years teach much which the days never knew."

— *Ralph Waldo Emerson*

People say to enjoy your children while they are little because they grow up so fast. I'm not so sure about that. Naturally I enjoy my children, at least most of the time. They are of average intelligence, usually pleasant and every now and then can be fun to be around. Not always of course, but they would likely say the same about me.

My oldest is 25 now and while I think it's great that I let him get that far along without putting him up for adoption or selling him to the gypsies, it really doesn't seem like it went by that fast. Someone said to me, "Can you believe it? He's 25, time flies!" I have no trouble believing it. I was there every day of those 25 years, living each fabulous minute of diapers, tantrums, school days, summers, teen years attitude and so much else. Does it seem like just yesterday he was 5 and going off to kindergarten? No, it doesn't. Honestly, it seems like it was a lifetime ago, because in a way, it was.

Andy went off to kindergarten with a backpack that was almost bigger than he was, a new pair of khakis and a crisp oxford shirt.

I was persuaded not to send him in a necktie — I saved that for picture day along with a lovely Harris Tweed blazer. Truly it's a wonder he speaks to me today. In my defense he was the first child. All of the ridiculous things first-time parents do, I did with him. It's like he was the practice kid.

At the end of that first school day — or, rather, three hours later, since he went to half-day kindergarten — he stumbled out of the classroom dragging his backpack, shirt untucked, leaves in his hair and holes in the knees of his Dockers. I thought maybe he had been beaten up or something because of my insistence on clothing better suited to a shoe salesman than a 5-year-old. Turns out he had just spent the day as all kids do, going full bore at the experience.

When he hit second grade, his brother was born and that's when the real fun began. He went from being the center of the universe to being the forgotten older sibling of his long-awaited baby brother who was never supposed to be. When he went to fifth grade, I was pregnant once again, with my third (and last!) child, and I'm not sure I even slowed the car down when I dropped him off on the first day. It's likely I would have needed a forklift to get myself and his cranky 3-year-old brother George out of the car.

Fifth-graders don't like to be seen with their parents anyway, so it was fine. The first day of school is a photo op when they are little, but frankly, by the time they hit middle school, most kids are more than happy to leap out of the car a block away from school and you really can't blame them.

The changes in them can't be seen every day; it takes years and that is how it should be. I saw my daughter in a little black dress, her first pair of heels and wearing lip-gloss as she left to attend a bat mitzvah for a friend and right there it was as if she was a whole other person. Not the baby of the family — that part is over. But it happened slowly, and I am glad of that.

I think the fact that I have three children makes it seem longer. You don't do the first day of school once; you do it three times. Teaching them to ride a two-wheeler, then to drive a car, go on a first date and eventually graduate is different with each of them, so maybe that is why it doesn't seem like it went by fast.

Just as those happy times are repeated with each child, so are the more challenging times. You know why only children are smarter and more successful? Because they never got yelled at and had their computer time taken away for smearing peanut butter in the hair of their younger brother or practicing Boy Scout first aid skills on their sister's Barbie dolls. I have spent more time than I care to think about refereeing petty squabbles about the unfairness of life. Apparently, my children were oppressed — by me, and definitely by each other. It is a wonder they survive from one day to the next having to constantly struggle to get their fair share of food, clothing and attention. To hear them tell it, they were practically refugees left to fend for themselves under a totalitarian overlord that never let them have any fun.

They don't even compete over the things I thought they would. Doesn't every kid want to be first at something? Not mine. They never worried about getting the first of something. They did, however, step all over each other to get the last of something. Apparently, if there is one Milano cookie left in the bag, they are convinced it is the last Milano cookie on the planet and their very survival depends on having it. I buy cookies all the time, but if there is one Milano and two children, that Milano then becomes an endangered species, unlikely to be seen again. Game on!

They are also expert observers of each other. We don't have a copy of it, but I often wonder if somewhere my kids got ahold of "The Art of War" by Sun Tzu. They know their opposition, and they know that the enemy of their enemy is their friend, so there are often alliances made between the three of them, usually in order to isolate the weakest (me) and thus gain the advantage of having or doing whatever it is that I've said no to. If my son spends time hanging out with a friend, my daughter wants to know what she gets to do. If my daughter goes shopping with me, my son wants to know if she got to spend time looking in the toy department and whether or not she got anything. Then next time I have to go to a store, he will insist on coming with me so the time is equal. My daughter has more shoes than he does, and while this isn't a problem for him, since he isn't that into shoes, he is aware of it and keeps that information on file for the next time the "it's not fair" issue comes up. When this kind of stuff is happening on a regular basis, the days can drag.

My children also like to compete with each other over how much they know. I wish a small part of that work ethic made it into their school assignments, but I understand why it doesn't. They don't want to be smarter than some kid that sits next to them. They want to know more than their siblings because that is power. One night over supper the word "supercalifragilisticexpialidocious" came up.

I am a world-class speller — it makes up for my dismal ability in math — and I asked the kids if they could spell it. Neither one could, but they both tried. One of them, I will not say who, declared victory because there was only one letter wrong in their attempt and the other kid had two letters wrong. When the oldest came home from school and talked about how he had almost beaten his friend at push-ups in gym class, doing 26 in a row, his younger brother dropped to the ground, did 26 push-ups and just for fun did four more...one-handed. And so it went, day after day.

I have a brother, so I know how this works. He is precisely 13 months older than I am, and he uses that to his advantage. It's only a little over a year, but my brother didn't let that stop him from using it any way he could. Every fall, his birthday comes along in October. He had the nerve to not only have been born a year before me, but in a month that comes right immediately before mine in the calendar year. I think mom liked him best. When he turned 10, he spent the next four weeks taunting me that he was now two years older than me, since I was still only 8. He is not now, nor will he ever be, two years older than I am, let's be clear on that. It was blatantly unfair, a gross miscarriage of justice, and I made sure I whacked him in the back of the head whenever I got the chance. Our mother never caught me doing this, because of the Second Man In theory. No one ever catches the first kid that does something, but they always catch the second one. I'd whack my brother, he'd chase me through the house and push me down; our mother would see it and nail him. Larry, you never realized it, but you got played.

Our parents always told us that we each got the same amount of everything. They played no favorites. I was convinced otherwise. After having my own kids, I finally figured it out. Separate but equal is not constitutional in terms of access to education, but it is perfectly acceptable in a family. A family is not a democracy. Nor should it be, if you ask me. The adults are in charge in my family. My children do not get an equal say in how our family works, and perhaps this is why they try so hard to outdo each other. It is their way of leveling the playing field; if they can't overrule me, they will do whatever they can to overrule each other.

Free speech is guaranteed under the Constitution, but so far I have not been hauled before the Supreme Court for infringing on the rights of my children when I settle an argument by telling them to zip it. I know this kind of competition is normal for their age, and it isn't going to stop anytime soon. It's what they do. It's what I did when my brother and I were growing up. But it will not divide them; they will not grow up to hate each other.

To this day I know for a fact that if my brother Larry thought for a minute someone was trying to hurt me, he would leap tall buildings to make it stop. And I would do the same. Nobody hits my brother but me.

My children may fight, but like Larry and I they will always have each other's backs. I have seen George practically spit nails at a kid who knocked his sister down by accident, and I saw my brother deck the kid who tried to steal my bike. My kids fight because they are related. And that is exactly why they will stand up for each other, too. It's family. If their squabbles have made the days seem long and the years stretch on then so be it.

I am not a perfect mother, nor would I want to be. While the days may have gone by slowly, they were never boring. I am fluent in sarcasm and hopefully my children will be too. Each day in our home there are wisecracks and thinly veiled insults along with everything else. I will not make motherhood seem like a Hallmark movie of the week, full of butterfly kisses and heart-shaped PB&Js. Depending on who you talk to raising kids can be nasty work, full of tears and torment or it can be sunshine and rainbows with happy snapshots of picnics and pony rides. What it mostly is though, is somewhere in the middle where if you're lucky they get to adulthood whole and healthy and without too much for their therapists to handle when they eventually become parents.

I don't know where exactly I fit or what kind of mother I am. It really depends on the day. Why are so many parents so worried about how they're doing? It's not like there's a report card. This is why our kids' teachers often roll their eyes at us; sometimes the parents are the toughest part of a teacher's job, not the kids. We truly need to get over ourselves. All this anxiety over whether or not we're doing it "right" will steal all the joy from the few times that do resemble a Hallmark moment. We all love our kids, to the moon and back. Hopefully we can provide them with a safe and happy home and enough food, clothes and fun to see them through the short years before we turn them loose on the world.

If you love your child, if you keep them safe as best you can, if you give them everything thing they need, if you make them laugh and sometimes make them cry, you're doing a great job. We resist labeling our kids, right? So why does it matter if you're a helicopter parent or an attachment parent, or a working parent? What kind of mother are you? What kind of dad? "What's it to you?" has always been my answer. I like labels on wine bottles; those are helpful. On parents? Not so much. The deep end of the carpool can be rough going, so why make it harder?

7

*"Life is like riding a bicycle. To keep your
balance, you must keep moving."*

— *Albert Einstein.*

Full disclosure, I don't have a clue about the meaning of life, what life is about or how we are all supposed to live it. No idea whatsoever. However, balance is something I've always strived for, and yet still have not quite managed. I think women especially struggle with balance, and I've never understood why that is. Perhaps it's because we are such good multi-taskers that everyone assumes that if you want something to go smoothly, your best bet is to ask a busy woman to handle it. Women have always been good at doing more than one thing at a time and staying on their toes, whether it's to reach the top shelf of the pantry where the stash of Hershey's kisses are hidden or it's managing a sales presentation, vacation Bible school and a bake sale all in the same day.

Balance is something that has eluded me for most of my fifty-odd years. Not the kind that requires managing a family, a job and a social life; it's going well on that front. This is largely due to having an excellent estrogen posse that keeps me laughing while navigating the deep end of the everyday responsibilities that are tiresome but necessary. The balance I lack is the kind that requires remaining upright while moving forward, i.e. walking. Falling down is something I do pretty often, and I've gotten really good at it. So far, there's been no need for bubble wrap and a football helmet, though friends have suggested both. It's an odd thing, but my feet, my brain and the ground have almost no connection to each other sometimes. It's like I'm one of those string puppets and someone took a scissors to the lines. When I was recovering from having my hip replaced (an unfortunate consequence of falling down is that your parts wear out a lot sooner) my physical therapist said, "For Christ's sake just don't fall down, I am not kidding." The new hip is ceramic. Since I can't always stay upright, anything breakable doesn't last long with me. I am the reason we can't have nice things at my house; almost no piece of crockery, china or glass has ever escaped my wrath. So putting a ceramic hip in the girl who can't keep her feet under her is a huge leap of faith. So far so good though; the hip remains unbroken and the goal is to keep it that way.

So balance was key during my recovery, but so was perseverance. At the same time some people were saying, "You got this, you go!" there were other people telling me to slow down and take it easy. So which is it? Slow down or keep going? Balancing those two ideas is harder than carrying a tray of martinis across a crowded room. My friends were great in the days after my surgery, helping out when I couldn't drive or even get in the shower on my own. Once driving was allowed, physical therapy took over my time and again the two concepts of moving forward while not overdoing it were at odds. This is where the wheels came off the walker for me. "Overdoing it" became wearing myself out going to the grocery store for milk and bread. Boy, pushing that carriage and hauling one measly bag to the car was a freaking endurance test. Patience is necessary for balance, another thing in short supply with me. My patience is right around that of a gnat on crack. The doctor and physical therapists were all over me about balance, about slowing down, about patience.

Can anyone tell me why patience is a virtue instead of "Hurry the hell up?" Slow and steady wins the race? Well, maybe in some kind of metaphorical way, but that's it. Races are won by the people who are faster than the ones limping along at the rear of the pack. I was perpetually cranky wanting to be off the crutches, done with the cane and back whacking away at badminton birdies, but it wasn't happening. There was a little progress, but it was painfully slow, and nothing makes me twitch more than having to wait for something. When I want something, I want it now, now now, let's get a move on people, step it up. Sounds delightful, doesn't it?

Then, my recovery hit a snag and it seemed all the progress that had been made was getting lost. Go backwards? Never. My father said to never look back, that wasn't where you were going. Also, knowing me as he did, he knew that if looked behind me I would likely bash into a wall I didn't see coming. Again the chorus of "slow down" was heard, which was well meant, but frustrating. It was beach season, if I had gone any slower a concerned team from Greenpeace might push me out to sea in a rescue attempt. Then, at a checkup at the surgeon's office, the issue was deemed resolved and a crisis was averted. He said, "Get back in the game. Do anything you want. Well, not anything. Don't skydive or go on a trampoline. Other than that, do whatever you want." Wait, what?

No more balance, no more "slow and steady?" The turtle was now supposed to become the hare? It was time to go full tilt, without actually tilting over and hitting the deck of course. What had been forgotten in the seemingly endless days of leg raises and rubber bands around my ankles is that my whole body needed to heal. Not just my big, fat Irish... hip. So then the plan became about hitting the gym every day, even if it was just a 15-minute stint on the treadmill. Swimming too, as much as I wanted. I was even cleared to ride my bike! Finally, a good reason to wear a helmet---a bike ride. I was still me though, so I kept the bike riding to the stationary bike in the gym.

Balance is necessary, no question. Working on one thing while ignoring other things is not balance though. Hyper-focusing on hip recovery wasn't balance it was tunnel vision. Being afraid to fall wasn't the issue; the fall had already happened. It was time to get back up. Up and down, back and forth, it's all good as long you keep moving and don't get caught in the undertow of the deep end.

Part two of the recovery then became all about forward motion, hitting it hard and kicking some butt. More than once my friends told me "Just keep swimming!" Oh, awesome, now it was a cartoon fish that knew everything about balance, perseverance and recovery? The problem is that when you've been limited for a while, as I had been after the hip surgery, you become a little gun shy. I was in crappy shape fitness-wise; I had been away from my beloved sport of badminton and for months a "workout" consisted of a few stretches and an ice pack. What if I looked silly waddling back into the gym in baggy sweats because none of my Lulus fit anymore? Quite frankly, I was embarrassed at how I looked, what I still couldn't do, and the mountain of work ahead of me to get back in some kind of reasonable shape.

Motivation will never be my forte. It is way too easy to find any excuse not to do the things we all know we should do. Finding a reason to skip something that likely isn't fun and doesn't pay off immediately is really easy. Oh, it's raining? Nope, can't go to the gym. Doesn't matter that it's indoors — it's raining, best to stay home in case the roof leaks. I've gone to a buy-one, get-one-free sale at my favorite shoe store in the middle of a blizzard, but driving to the gym in the rain? That doesn't happen. It's hard to be motivated when it seems like the list of things you can't do is miles longer than the list of those you can. That's when you have to be Scarlett O'Hara. If something is hard or difficult? Well, you just think about that tomorrow. It doesn't matter what it is, just put that aside and think about what you can do.

I started with my game. I came late to finding a sport I loved, but badminton was it. The reason I took to it had to be because of the women who taught me how to play. They didn't mind that I had no idea where to stand or how to keep score. It wasn't a problem that most of the time I couldn't get the bird over the net. They showed up every week and they gave me this game, they gave me something I'd never had before: a sport. Were there embarrassing moments when I first started? Absolutely. The falling down thing didn't just go away because I had a racket and a new pair of shoes. There is nothing like going for a smash at the net and winding up flat on your back on the court during your first tournament. It wasn't all in my head, people were actually staring, and a few were laughing. Just keep swimming? Sure, that helps when you've just gone arse over teakettle in front of a hundred or so people. The fact that I'd been down before, though? That did help. People who have never dog-paddled their way out of a rip tide aren't the ones who know what the deep end is really like.

I'd been knocked on my backside for sure, but failure doesn't have to be fatal. Unless you screw up flying a plane or something, then you might have a problem, but otherwise, not so much. Bad hips happen, so does cancer, and being out of shape and just falling down and bashing your knee bloody. It all happens, and it's all just another bump in the road.

Fortunately I grew up in an Irish Catholic home, and self-pity and petty gripes were not well tolerated, so while I might not always be motivated, I do make sure that what needs to be done gets done...eventually. When I would complain about having green beans at supper when I was little, my mother didn't use the old "starving children in Africa" example, but she did threaten to send me up to South Boston to live with my Uncle Jack's family. They had an apartment, no yard, and no beach at the end of the street, and all five of my cousins had to share one bike since there was no room to store any more than that. I still wouldn't eat the green beans, but I had the good sense to shut up about them. Which was probably my mother's goal.

SINK OR SWIM: TALES FROM THE DEEP END OF EVERYWHERE

Things could always be worse, right? That's hardly profound, but the truth is they could always be better too, but no one ever says that. We have all had some tough hits; it's part of life. My father, Frank Kelley, was convinced that things would always get better. No matter how bad a situation was he just knew that it would improve. He was a child of the Great Depression, but you'd never know it by him. Rather than having been beaten down by poverty and hard times, he remained optimistic that better days were coming. Remember the old joke about the kid on Christmas who asked for a pony but woke up to a pile of horse manure under the tree and said, "With this much horse shit, there must be a pony around here somewhere?" My father was that kid. Even if you were wading knee deep in crap, better days were just around the corner. I think of him every time I find myself in deep water because he reminds me that the shore is always in reach.

It happens, though it absolutely does, those better days do arrive. Maybe they don't bring a pony, but days when the mile time on the treadmill at the gym comes out just a bit shorter than it was last time eventually come. Days when the jeans fit, the hip didn't hurt and a badminton drop shot went sailing over the net finally came for me. And eventually a day when those same hundred or so people that saw me go on my butt on the badminton court stood up and cheered for me and handed me a trophy for winning my first tournament.

Every day is a reset. Every day there is another excuse or another trip to the gym. The difference is motivation, and it doesn't always last. What moves us forward will change with every step, but we have to keep looking for it.

8

"He who would travel happily must travel light"

----- Antoine de Saint-Exupéry

Traveling light is more of a goal for me than an actual reality. The intention is always to pack light; it just never seems to turn out that way. It started when I was little and there was this big bag that must have been a briefcase of my father's. It was magical to me; there were so many things that would fit in the different sections. It was filled with my dolls, pads of paper, crayons and usually some snacks, and I would lug it with me everywhere. Then when Easter rolled around each year I would get a purse. There was always an outfit to wear for church, usually something spring-like, but it was not Easter unless there was a purse to go with it. When Santa brought a doll carriage for Christmas one year, there was room for even more stuff, and I pushed the carriage around full of my treasures while dragging the case and my purse as well. Hopefully that wasn't a glimpse of my old age, pushing a cart around with all my worldly goods in it. I don't know why I needed to carry so much stuff around with me, but it's a habit that's very hard to break.

SINK OR SWIM: TALES FROM THE DEEP END OF EVERYWHERE

When it was time to pack up and go off to college, of course I took damn near everything I owned. Even the tennis racket that had never been out of my closet was loaded into the car full of the essentials. I didn't play tennis then, nor do I play now, but that racket went to Vermont with me that first year. Just in case!

That is what sabotages my attempts to pack light, the whole "just in case" concept. Traveling is great fun. The point is to go places you haven't been, to see new things and have different experiences. How can you pack light if you have no way of knowing what you might run into? So what if you are going skiing in Maine in December? What if there's a heat wave? You might need peep-toe pumps and a cute sundress. The Boy Scouts are all about being prepared, but after seeing the very basic supply list for my son's Boy Scout camp last summer, I'm not so sure. Nowhere on that list did it suggest bringing along plastic drinking straws or a set of dice, but those can come in handy, trust me.

I was talking with a friend who has spent 25 years in the military. He has been deployed all over the world, sometimes with less than a few hours notice. He told me he could pack everything he would need for a six-month stint overseas into a duffle bag, and it would take 10 minutes. Well, good for him. I'm willing to bet he wore the same outfit every day, you know, a uniform? And it's likely he never needed to take a pair of trendy beaded sandals for the beach, sneakers for comfort and a little strapless number for going out to a romantic restaurant. Somehow I can't picture him needing a black camisole to go under a silk blouse, two hairbrushes and three kinds of moisturizer.

If you are an "OOPS" like I am though (Obsessive Over-Packing Savant) the key is to know how to get the most amount of stuff into the smallest bag. We OOPS travelers never check bags. That is for amateurs. What if the airline loses your bag? All that preparation for any possible scenario goes down the drain. On a road trip you need space for blankets and pillows and fast food bags, so the suitcase has to be small. Roll things up, stick socks in corners and make sure you wear the bulky stuff. You might look a little lumpy, but if you can wear a turtleneck, a heavy sweater, jeans, a blazer and hiking boots, there will be enough room in your bag for the really important stuff like swim goggles and an extra umbrella. Packing light is overrated. There are so many things that could happen on a trip that taking extra stuff is the smart way to go.

So now that you're packed, if it's a road trip there are some rules. I've survived several car trips to Philadelphia and Maryland in the dog days of August. Who needs the cool breezes of Nantucket or the Cape? Philly in August is how we roll. I figure I will need to practice for all the time I'm probably going to spend in hell, and this seems like the best way. It's a pretty long trip and this is what I've learned.

Always bring a bucket. A jar with a lid is a goo idea too. Nothing is worse than having to clean up the splatter of projectile bodily fluids with the five or six Dunkin' Donuts napkins you have in the glove box. The jar comes in handy for avoiding the rest-area bathrooms. I was told it's also a good way to tell if your kid really needs to pee or just wants another stop on the Great Bathroom Tour of America. If they are willing to go in the jar, pull over.

Bring the technology. We all moan about how our kids spend too much time plugged into their games and devices but I know my kids. Eight hours on the road is excruciating if some part of the trip isn't dedicated to tech time. Preferably with all family members in separate headphone sets. License-plate bingo and family sing-alongs should be avoided at all costs.

Watch the road rage. Different parts of the country have different driving habits. I'm told in some states people actually signal before they change lanes. Speed limits are actually enforced in other parts of the country, unlike in Massachusetts where speed limits are theoretical and traffic lights are seen as suggestions. I can usually curb my language around the kids, but sometimes a driving situation gets the best of me and I let loose with the words my mother learned in the Navy and passed on to me. I try my best to keep quiet and get along with my fellow drivers however keeping the language clean means that at times, in an effort to be peaceful, I have resembled the Gandhi of the single finger gesture. Thanks to a high school friend I am also fluent in several Italian hand gestures.

Road trips can be fun or they can be torture; it's mostly up to the adults to send it one way or another, so be ready. But what if you fly? Everything about going on a plane is fun for me. What's not to like? The first time I went to Ireland, the plane lifted off from Boston at sunset, and the view out of the tiny window was of Boston harbor with the Prudential and the Hancock buildings silhouetted against pink and purple clouds.

Landing at Shannon was at sunrise with emerald green squares of farmland coming up out of the clouds. If that isn't a miracle of our modern world, then I don't know what is. Planes are magic!

I've always liked watching planes come and go. My father would take me to Castle Island in South Boston every summer for fried clams, and we would watch the planes headed for Logan. I attended Saint Michael's College in beautiful Winooski, VT and the campus was practically on the approach to the airport. Along with the usual air traffic, there F-4 fighter jets screamed overhead from the Vermont Air National Guard. Admittedly this took some getting used to, but after the first week I no longer threw myself to ground because I thought one of them was landing in the quad.

A good friend was in the Air Force ROTC program and got word one day that a C-5 cargo plane would be doing a "touch and go" at the airport. I remember piling into a car and racing to a back road that bordered the runway to watch it come in. That is one huge plane, and seeing it up close was amazing.

There is a playground that my brother took my kids to when they were very little, and it's a favorite now because it looks across the bay to the runways at Logan. When my daughter is on the swings, she thinks the planes are close enough to touch. It has a name, but we just call it "Airplane Park." I am never happier than when I can see the ocean, the city of Boston and planes, and this place has it all.

However, not everyone feels this way, and I get that. For some, air travel is a pain in the neck. It's security lines and baggage fees and cramped seating. No argument here, all of that is part of getting on a plane now. So what? Those are minor details when you think about the fact that you can get all the way across an ocean, all the way across our country, in basically an afternoon. So maybe we need a few tips to make it a little easier. If I were Queen of All Things — or as my coffee mug says, "She Who Must Be Obeyed" — I would set up some rules.

Be ready for security. The Ziploc bags and tiny bottles of shampoo might be a drag, but just do it. Unless you're vacationing in Kosovo you can likely just buy a few toiletries when you arrive. Keep it simple, and for the sake of those behind you don't wander up to security wearing a pair of riding boots with six buckles, 27 bangle bracelets and a purse the size of Rhode Island.

Be nice to the flight attendants. Maybe back in the day they were there to look cute and pour drinks, but not anymore. Their job is to make sure you're safe. If anything happens on a flight, they know how to pop a slide and get your sorry butt off that plane, whether it's on fire, in the water or just hits the ground too hard. They serve drinks, but they can save your life, too, which kind of makes them like my most favorite people ever, firefighters in the grocery store. Think about it for a second: Firefighters are cute as hell, they can cook, and they won't let you burn to death on their watch. The flight attendants are in the same league if you ask me and they deserve your respect and courtesy.

Size matters. You can't fit a suitcase the size of a coffee table in an overhead bin. If you are the size of an NBA point guard and your head is scraping the roof of the plane, be careful when you recline your seat. I know it's cramped and you can't help being 6'6", but how about requesting the exit row where there's a little more room? There's limited space on a plane; everyone needs to suck it in a little.

So, now hopefully you've arrived safely at your destination and it's time to have some fun. This is what you've saved for, planned for and waited for. The best piece of advice I've ever gotten is to go big or stay home. This was my father's favorite thing to say and it was never about money or first class plane tickets or expensive hotels. It was about making the trip an experience. Even if it's a business trip, go somewhere out of the ordinary. Don't go to Rome and eat at McDonalds. Find the little local place off the beaten path. Think about it, are you going to spend money, pack your bags, deal with planes, trains and automobiles all so you can have dinner at Applebee's?

Why go anywhere if all you see are the same things you see at home? Talk to people you've never met, dip your toes in the fountain and sing on the tour bus. Just be careful what you sing. I had a friend who got kicked out of the Ritz Hotel bar for singing Irish pub tunes, and it was unpleasant. There's no need to ruin the trip by acting out, but isn't the reason you're on vacation because you wanted to change things up?

While going native is fun, don't skip all the tacky tourist things. I don't care how old I am, I will always be giddy when I get to meet a Disney character. Going to Legoland was for the kids, but I had a blast too. They have an entire replica of the Las Vegas strip, all in Legos. Posing for goofy pictures with Lego brick people taller than me? Sign me up. I even got to see Pierce Brosnan's star on Hollywood's Walk of Fame. I may have swooned, just a little. My kids pretended not to know me, but I'm used to that. I left a little note for Pierce, and I'm certain he's going to call me.

Traveling takes us away from the everyday, to new places, both on the road and within ourselves. Be nice to those you meet along the way. Tip well, have dessert and buy something stupidly funny that you don't really need. A friend of mine never says goodbye if someone she knows is leaving on a trip. She simply tells them "Come back happy!" The best way to keep from sinking is to paddle your way over to another part of the world and see what the water is like over there.

9

"Snips and snails and puppy dog tails that's what little boys are made of. Sugar and spice and all things nice that's what little girls are made of."

--Author Unknown

Does anyone else cringe when they hear this? Perhaps the present day version is "Boys will be boys" or "Run like a girl." Also cringe-worthy if you ask me. Just how does a girl run? I suppose you could ask Shalane Flanagan...if you can catch her. Boys will be boys? OK, what does that mean other than they won't be llamas, pumpkins or wildebeest? There's a lot of stuff out there that's defined by and targeted to gender and it just seems pointless to me in this modern world.

When I went to first grade, back in the Stone Age, the school building had separate entrances for boys and girls. Built into the façade of the building, carved in granite, there was a little boy face over one door, and a little girl face over the other. No matter what, boys and girls entered and exited the building separately. Because you know what first grade boys and girls are like. Get them near each other and who knows what could happen.

I remember walking to school with my brother and when we got there, he went to his door and I went to mine. Sure, it would probably have been like that anyway, but we never questioned it and looking back, it's amazing I stood for it. I was kicked out of preschool because I told the teacher, in no uncertain terms, that her schedule wasn't working for me. When it was circle time I thought we should go out, when it was snack time I wanted to paint, and when it was time for a nap, I thought it should be time to sing songs. I lasted two days before they told my mother it "wasn't the right fit." But two years later, in first grade, I was lining up by gender and not saying a word about it.

It's different today of course. Boys and girls, men and women, all of us mix up together any way we like now. As it should be. There are no separate entrances in public schools, gym class is co-ed and in some universities dormitories are shared by men and women and there's nothing wrong with any of that that. It was a bit of surprise when I went back to the dorm I'd lived in at Saint Michael's College and found two men in my old room. Back in the day, there would have been a big fat hairy deal over two men in the women's dorm. The stereotypes aren't completely gone though. There are a few things that still make me stop and wonder if I've been kidnapped by a time lord and send back a few decades.

Browsing Twitter, I came across a picture that a friend posted of the magazine section in a local store in her area. Shelves held copies of every magazine you could imagine. What was right above the rack? The store had put up signs and labeled different sections of the display "Men's Interests" and "Women's Interests." That's when I went a little deaf for a second from the screeching inside my head. Seriously, why is that necessary? But wait, there's more.

The only thing worse than having magazines sorted by what someone in marketing thinks men and women are interested in was the specific titles they put in those sections. For no discernible reason the Men's section had *Runners World*, *Consumer Reports*, *Popular Science* and *Boston Magazine*.

SINK OR SWIM: TALES FROM THE DEEP END OF EVERYWHERE

You hear that ladies? Stop reading all of those. I don't care what your mile time is, how much you want to know about the schools around Boston or what you need to research about the next television you want to buy. Those are not for you. What's that? You're a biologist at Harvard and you want to read the latest science news? No, sorry. *Popular Science* is for men. Women, even those in the field of science and technology, don't need to read any of that, at least according to whoever set up the sections.

For the ladies it was *Food and Wine*, *Vanity Fair* and *Bon Apetit* among others. The lead article in the issue of *Vanity Fair* was about two guys who were the first to free climb Yosemite's Dawn Wall. There was also an article about the Wall Street banking crisis of 2008. Sorry guys, none of you manly men want to read about that right? *Bon Apetit* had an article about craft beer, but everyone knows men don't drink beer, right?

Adding insult to injury, there were snacks in this section, also organized into the Men's and Women's categories. The chocolate was on the men's side and the bags of chips and nuts were on the women's. How stupid is that? Women need chocolate and no man wants his nuts anywhere near *Oprah Magazine*.

That's what happens when some arbitrary marketing strategy goes too far. Yes, of course no one is stopping a guy from buying *Star Magazine* or a woman from grabbing *ESPN Monthly*; it's about the message it sends to kids, because believe me, they notice this stuff. It's a message that says girls don't like sports or science and boys don't want to read about opening a restaurant or winning Top Chef. Here's a novel concept. How about the magazines get arranged alphabetically, like in the library? We all know the alphabet right? If it has to be topics, keep it simple: Food, Fashion, Home Décor, Sports, Technology, and Entertainment.

This isn't the crime of the century of course, but this kind of divide is all over the place. There was a cute recipe for Lego brownies on a website I was surfing around, (colored frosting and M&Ms make them look like the bricks) and the caption under it said, "Moms, whip these up for your boy's birthday party, they'll be a hit." That's because no girls like Legos, right? Brownies get "whipped up" by moms, never by dads, also a universal truth. Brownies, magazines, toys, books, it's just ridiculous how needlessly segregated it still is.

Yes, males and females are different; I get that. They shop and spend in different ways too, that's been shown in countless studies. It's when you start separating out information according to gender that you lose me. I read *Boston Magazine* all the time, so now it's like Irish Spring? "Manly yes, but I like it too!" That's just crazy. Everyone should read more; even the trashy magazines give us an escape. Who doesn't need more chicken recipes? A person's gender doesn't belong in the magazine section; it belongs in underwear

Nowhere is this gender divide more comical than on Valentine's Day. It's kind of a ridiculous holiday, but somehow it's become more than just one day, it's an entire retail season. The best card I ever saw poked fun at the whole concept because it read, "I don't understand why Cupid was chosen to represent Valentine's Day. When I think about romance, the last thing on my mind is a short, chubby toddler coming at me with a weapon." Maybe I'm just cranky, but I think it's a big waste of time.

I asked a lot of my friends about Valentine's Day and what they thought because perhaps I was wrong, and people really do like it. I asked men and women, both single and married. It was not a scientific poll of any kind, and the results are not anything more than a collection of opinions, but I was a little shocked at the outcome. It's not just me! Not one person I asked really likes this Hallmark holiday. But their reasons were different and, as expected, fell along gender lines and to a certain extent marital status.

The men all felt that it was a made up holiday and was, in the words of one male acquaintance, "fraught with peril." They all agreed that yes, it was expected of them to buy a card, flowers, candy or gifts, but even if they did, they feared they might still fall short. The men I spoke to wanted to do the right thing, but seemed unsure of what exactly that was. Honestly, isn't that how it is every day for men? This kind of stuff eludes a lot of them. It's not their fault we women are light years ahead of them emotionally. OK, OK, that's not entirely true. Men are not completely stunted in this area, but they struggle sometimes, and that's not a problem. As long as they try (and can also kill bugs and fix things), most women don't mind that much.

The men I spoke with bravely admitted to some stress over the whole thing. Should they send a funny card, or a serious, romantic card? If they bought candy, would their women folk think it was insensitive to their efforts to stay in shape? If they didn't buy candy, was that sending a message that their wives could stand to lose a few pounds? The stuffed-animal question is difficult as well. Do adult women really want red-and-white teddy bears?

Finally, there is the jewelry issue. Some of the men I know were just getting out of the dog house from Christmas, both financially and personally. One poor, misguided friend of mine had purchased a crock-pot for his wife for Christmas. He was pretty sure that nothing short of diamonds was going to get him out of the hole, and credit-card debt was a small price to pay

Not surprisingly, single men were not bothered by Valentine's Day as much as some single women were. For a single man, it's like getting a bye week. That is a sports term, which involves a team getting a week off and somehow still making it into the playoffs. I don't actually know any more than that about a bye week, but a guy I know said it's a good analogy. For the men I spoke with, being single on Valentine's Day means you live to fight another day. You get to point and laugh at your friends who are in the supermarket late on the night of the 13th. The aisles are clogged with men who have partners, wives and girlfriend and they're agonizing over the choice between the hip Hershey's Kisses or the ever popular but somewhat outdated heart-shaped box with the tacky ribbon and the soft centered candy everyone's grandmother likes. The single men get to snicker and mumble, "Yo, dude... sucks to be you."

As for the women, well, it kind of depends. Women that were single told me they didn't like the reminders everywhere that the whole world is supposed to be paired up with the love of their lives. Single women feel left out. Think about it. Even the little kids in school come home with valentines and miniature chocolate hearts.

Their married or partnered up co-workers and friends get flowers or go out to dinner, and the single girls find themselves at home eating a tube of cookie dough and watching Lifetime, a.k.a., "television for women and the men they hate."

The married or otherwise engaged women I talked with really liked the romance aspect of the holiday, but as a rule they were not concerned with the date. Women like their partners to get romantic, to send mushy cards and bring flowers or little gifts. What's not to like about that? However, most of us are fine with it happening on some random Tuesday in October. In fact, more than a few women told me that the little "for no reason" surprises they had gotten over the years meant more to them than the candy and flowers they may have only gotten out of a sense of obligation and fear.

So men, take note: it's a little bit of a gamble. You can keep up with it on a regular basis, and it's easy and fun. Or you can put it off and try to cram it all into one high-stakes day. You just have to ask yourselves one question: "Do I feel lucky?" Well, do ya?

It's only one day. Twenty-four hours. All this drama and fuss isn't necessary. It doesn't honor our mothers and fathers. It's not a sacred religious day. It's not when we pause to remember those who gave their lives in the service of their country. It's just some silly fun. Whether you are married or single, a man or a woman, just think of it as the one day of the year when nobody will laugh if you walk around with a heart on.

Men and women, boys and girls, it's all just a big joke I think. We're all different, but not because we are male or female. It's because we are human.

10

"Let's dare to be ourselves, for we do that better than anyone else can."

— *Shirley Briggs*

That's the standard advice we always hear, right? Just be yourself! We tell our kids that all the time when they insist on having the same clothes and gear that all their friends have. "Be yourself, not some copy of someone else." It's sound advice, too. Nothing good can come of trying to be something you're not; eventually people see through it and then you just look like a fake. Being genuine isn't easy in a sea of carbon copies, but it's so worth it.

There is an exception, though. One place where being completely real is not actually expected. Social media. Who are we kidding? No one's life is really how it looks a Facebook page. It's not that we are all lying about ourselves, not at all. We just like to put the good stuff on display in ways we never would in a face-to-face conversation.

Let's back it up before Facebook though. A few years ago, some of my friends were into scrapbooking. There's nothing wrong with that; they made beautiful photo albums for their kids. However, one friend, with whom I've lost touch, was having a hard time in her life. Her marriage was ending, and there were problems with her children. However, her Christmas letter contained three scrapbook pages with pictures of outings to the aquarium and picnics in the park. Did she take her kids to these events so everything would look fine? I always wondered how she dealt with the parts of her life that didn't fit neatly into a Creative Memories layout. I wish I had known she was struggling; maybe I could have helped.

Then Facebook comes along, and my newsfeed is filled with everyone's graduation pictures, prom pictures, and moving-into-college pictures. Hell, if someone had something yummy for lunch, they posted it! Myself included. For me, it's like the cyberspace version of the old movie "Rear Window", without actually witnessing a murder. I get to see what all my friends are doing, what their kids are up to or what kind of new dog they just got. It's nice to be able to celebrate with people I don't get to see every day, but there is a limit. Just like when I've had enough sweets and my teeth start to hurt, there is a point where it hits critical mass and everyone's perfect little worlds are just too much to take in.

Just once, I would like to open up Facebook and see someone post about the burnt apple pie that set off the smoke alarm, or the coffee that spilled all over the car. Instead of seeing someone's auto post from an exercise app that reads "Suzie ran five miles in 45 minutes and feels great. Rock on!" I would like to read "Suzie stayed home from the gym today and ate six Oreos because her jeans are tight anyway, so does it even matter? Suzie feels like a heifer. Moo!"

That never happens though, does it? Or it could be that all of my friends really do have Kodak moments every day and never burn the pie or spill the coffee. I have some awesome friends; it's entirely possible. What is not possible, however, is that other shiny happy corner of social media: Pinterest. Holy inferiority complex, Batman; those people are just not real.

I spent some time checking it out, and I have to conclude that I am just not worthy. Either that, or everyone there is a big fat liar.

When you sign up, you have to "follow" five boards to get started. I chose social media, hairstyles, humor, tattoos and recipes. I figured I would stick with things I either have (tattoos, a sense of humor and social media) or want to know more about (hairstyles and recipes). I have no idea how they decide to configure the layout of all that, but when I opened up my main feed it looked like the Internet had puked all over my Mac. Right next to what looked like some delicious homemade donuts was a tattoo of a monkey's butt centered on someone's navel. I may never eat another donut. The random stuff all over the screen was just a violent sensory barrage for me. I'm as ADD as the next person, but it was way too scattered to even take in, so I must be doing it wrong.

That seems to be the message on Pinterest, though. We're all doing it wrong, except whoever those perfect people are that pin the craft ideas and the eerily over-posed kid pictures. You think a first day of school snapshot of your kids in the yard with their new backpacks is all you need to do? Oh no. It's way past that. I saw a pinned item that was a picture of a kid in front of a blackboard that read, "First day of 3-year-old Kindy." Let's be clear about something: Grown adults don't call it "Kindy," and 3-year-olds don't go to anything remotely resembling kindergarten. Cut the crap. It's preschool or nursery school; hell, it's daycare. Let's not overthink it.

Women make up 97% of Pinterest users. Shocker, right? No. Most men wouldn't be caught dead pinning scented-candle arrangements and cappuccino foam designs. They have lives to lead, empires to run and fantasy football rosters to create. Men don't care what other men do unless it involves their dream teams or their actual food.

Why do women spend time and energy on this stuff? Aren't we busy enough? We have jobs and families and, you know, functioning brain cells.

Who are these women with this kind of time? I think they are likely the same women that create impossibly cute bento-box lunches for their kids complete with uplifting hand-written notes on organically recycled napkins that say, "You're special!"

Ladies, I am begging you; I just can't live up to that standard. Can someone please create a board on Pinterest and call it "Things I Suck At" and pin some pictures of a forgotten pizza box in an oven? What about the Halloween costume disaster that was supposed to be a cow but was really just a sweatshirt with felt dots falling off it? I can't be the only woman that has one of those in the back of her closet. Chalk painting furniture seems to be a big deal on these boards, but somehow I don't think that a snapshot of my coffee table with the alphabet written in sidewalk chalk all over the top would fit in with the rest of the items.

Pinterest is billed as an inspirational medium, a place to get ideas and share common interests. I'm not seeing it, but I'm going to keep looking. Maybe there's a board full of "Pinterest Fails," and that's where all the real people are? That must be it because it's just not possible that thousands of people want to drink lemonade out of a mason jar at a wedding or design gift baskets for Letter Carrier Appreciation Day. I'm calling BS on that.

The other part of social media that's definitely a reality disconnect is the fact that every urban legend or myth now has new life. The Internet is a powerful tool, and it's part of the world we live in, but it can be a vehicle for rumors and half-truths as well. These kinds of stories have always been there, but somehow because it's online, more people believe them. How is that possible?

Anatole France said, "*If 50 million people say a foolish thing, it is still a foolish thing.*" There are hundreds of millions of people using the Internet and it's a safe bet that a good percentage of them are spewing nothing but foolishness. So why does it work, why do people continue to believe something because they see it on a screen?

I've lost count of the times that dozens of people told me something, all of them swearing up and down it was 100% true, and it turned out to be not only foolish, but just outright fiction. I was headed to the airport once at the start of a vacation and a storm was coming. My trip went fine, the reports were way off, but the weather forecasters were going on like it was the end of days. From the terminal I watched at least three news reporters broadcasting about the impending storm, advising people to do everything but build an ark, because surely the world was going to end.

It didn't —just like it didn't end in December 2012 when everyone was all worked up about the Mayan calendar. But if you were cruising around the Internet in December 2012, it was all anyone could talk about. Even NASA got into the debate because of planetary alignments and the fact that the Sun's December solstice happened to fall on the very day the Mayan calendar ended. Well we know how that worked out, the world still turns, but people still believe a lot of what they see online, strictly because it's online.

So how do we know what to believe and what not to believe in this information age? Carl Sagan said, *"Finding the occasional straw of truth awash in a great ocean of confusion and bamboozle requires intelligence, vigilance, dedication and courage."* How much of that do we normally see on the Internet or in the political ads, the debates and the elections? Not enough, not nearly enough.

Open up Facebook on any given day and you will see posts about deadly vaccinations, airline giveaways, rapists in mall parking lots and get-rich-quick schemes. What amazes me though, is the gullibility factor. People who I thought were pretty tech savvy have at one time or another posted those ridiculous warnings about Facebook owning any content you put up on your page. Then there were the posts about Mark Zuckerberg picking a select few users to give his millions to, as a thank you. Mark himself went on television to say it wasn't happening, and yet the herd of online sheep continued to baa baa baa themselves into a full-on frenzy. Posts began with "Well it couldn't hurt to try" but the thing is, it does hurt. Every time someone posts one of these urban myths our collective intelligence takes a hit. Also, I heard that a unicorn dies and some kid who needs a heart transplant doesn't get one if you don't also share their picture along with your note of thanks to Mark Z.

The giveaways are fake. The scary stories about fingers found in fast food are fake. The science on vaccinations causing autism is fake too, and so are all the posts that promise a free trip to Disney World just for liking and sharing a picture of Mickey. When it's just a bunch of stories it's one thing, but the political process has been affected as well. Rather than getting to know a candidate's position on an issue, many people see something online, in an email forward or other media, and make a decision without checking any facts. Pictures are Photoshopped to make the rumor of the week seem authentic, but lots of people don't bother to really check out a story. It was online, so it must be true.

The Internet can be a wonderful source for knowledge, but we elected 42 presidents before it became the unstoppable political machine it is now. Were there still millions of people saying foolish things back in the day? Of course there were, we just didn't have to hear all of them. Thank you Twitter, Drudge, Gawker and the rest. The Internet hasn't made us any smarter; it has simply made us louder.

The Internet and politics are just a part of the picture. Rumors and unbelievable stories make up a lot of what we see and hear every day and that is a real issue. Everyone. No one. Always. Never. Those are pretty powerful words. Even more so for our kids. They're the pioneers of all this social media, they practically invented it, but they might be the most vulnerable to it as well. If they believe everything they hear, what kind of choices will they make? If "everyone" is doing something dangerous, will they be able to stay safe? The deep end of the teenage years can be a tough go. The tide of misinformation can carry them under and no one wants that to happen.

The challenge is to weed out the foolish and find the better ideas, and that is especially difficult for our young people. I wouldn't be a junior or senior in high school again if you paid me. Well, except for prom night, that was pretty nice. But the rest? No thank you. It was hard enough then, and I had a pretty easy time of it considering.

We have grown adults, in leadership positions, with years of education and experience, and they don't always get it. How are the kids supposed to? I mean, we tell them the right things, but do they listen? They do not. Maybe they have to learn the hard way, but they should know one thing even Forrest Gump had no trouble understanding: stupid is as stupid does. And that goes for everyone, adults included.

11

"No party is any fun unless seasoned with folly."

---Desiderius Erasmus

While it might be morbid to think about, on my tombstone, if they still have tombstones when I die, I would like the inscription to say, "Loved a party, never minded a drink." It's simple but it says it. Not that I'm some kind of party animal, because that's not the case at all. In my younger days I had my fill of the pub crawls, keggers and all night wanderings with my girlfriends. I've waited in line outside of clubs, hit the road on a whim because I got last minute concert tickets and I've chowed down at a Waffle House at 3am, because when it's that time of night and you're hungry and headed for daylight and regrets, big greasy pancakes are the answer. While I'm a modern girl and I love my tech and online reality, I am also glad my college years happened before everyone had a smartphone in their pocket. Somewhere a blurry Fotomat print exists of me in someone's dorm room with the cardboard boxes from two six packs of Michelob on my head, but it's never going to see the light of day if I have my way.

Now that I'm a full-fledged adult, the term "party" is very different. Celebrations in this part of my life are about more than just the fact that it's Friday at 3pm. There's a season to it, and the events come and go during the year. The holidays in the winter have everyone running around getting ready to host dinners and family. Gifts have to be purchased for friends, for hosts and the ever-popular Yankee swap parties. Then there's a break and it starts over with Easter, the beginning of spring for some, and continues through Mother's Day, Memorial Day, Father's Day, proms, graduations and then July 4th with its fireworks and back yard barbeques. Not a weekend seems to go by when there isn't a reason to celebrate something. There's a bit of a lag after Independence Day and before the last summer blow out of Labor Day, so one summer I chose that stretch to throw a party.

It had been hectic time at my house, but not with holiday parties. The same long stretch that had been full of fireworks and BBQs elsewhere, was, for me, focused on recovering from surgery, physical therapy, packing one kid for a summer job in another state, and keeping the other kid from becoming a casualty of summer boredom. There was a prom in there, and that was definitely the highlight. It was a privilege to see my son George decked out in a tuxedo and escorting a lovely friend to the dance. The school did a red carpet and I was definitely the psychotic mom snapping photos there, and of course before the prom in my yard, the date's yard, and even some stranger's yard that we drove by. Hey, it had better flowers than our garden and even if he did scream about he got out of the car and stood next to those hydrangeas. It was crazy busy most of the time, with one to-do list item after another in place of the parties all my friends were going to.

Well enough of that noise, I needed a party. As with anything, if you want it done right, you do it yourself. For what though? What was the occasion? It was two weeks into August before I things slowed down and as it happens August is the only month without a national holiday. It seemed there was nothing to have a party about. Then a red leather couch came along and we were in business. A little backstory. Some years before,

I had bought a couch from a little old lady who was moving to Boca. It was a gorgeous shade of red leather and she was the sweetest person for letting me having it for almost no money, which was exactly what I had at the time. The problem was I had nothing to go with it. For years I was on the lookout to find something to go with this beautiful red couch. I had kept an old green loveseat that should have been tossed out long ago, but between the toys and the kiddy furniture my living room started to look like Santa Claus lived there. Little by little though, the toys got weeded out and the stuffed animals were sent on their way to new homes. But still, nothing had been found to match the red couch, which I steadfastly refused to give up because it was so gorgeous.

Then one day, in a little corner of Craigslist, there was my answer. Someone was selling the exact same red leather couch that I had. I jumped on that baby like a cricket on crack and it was mine. My brother was coerced into delivering it and with a little rearranging, what appeared before me? A living room that looked like grown-ups lived there. Matching couches practically scream "responsible adult." There were curtains on the windows and my grandmother's Waterford on the shelves. If that isn't a reason for a party, I don't know what is.

So the call went out to my friends, and yes, we are talking just the girls here. Who else would celebrate a couch? Chick chat, with wine and snacks for Happy Red Couch Day! Finally, one room in my home no longer looked like the set of a Nickelodeon show. Naturally, there were preparations to be made. Food and beverages were purchased, the floor was swept (ok, not really) and I took the cases of pasta and toilet paper out of the dining room and stored them where they are supposed to go. Every wine glass I owned was on the table, no two of them alike, pictures were hung and candles were lit. That is when the panic set in.

Happy Red Couch Day? What was I thinking? People don't have parties for couches, and hello, what about the rest of my house? While I love my little cottage by the sea, it is by no means an environment of beauty. One look at the almost-bare walls and the hardwood floors that have seen better days (and two dogs), and you just know that Town and Country isn't coming by for a photo shoot anytime soon. It's clean, sometimes, it's safe, and it's happy, but it's not spacious or elegant.

I shouldn't have worried. The thing is, while it's only a couch and only one room, I have the kind of friends who totally get it. None of them minded that the rest of the house was in a bit of disarray. None of them thought it was weird that a garage sale couch was a big deal for me. While it's usually impolite to talk price, I have to brag; the couch was $100 and it was practically brand new. Hell, yes, that is a reason to celebrate.

I will always be a fan of finding something ordinary and fun to celebrate and calling some friends in for a toast and a nibble. If you think about it hard enough, there's always a reason to celebrate friendship and a happy home with good food and drink.

That's what friends of mine did one bright summer day. They hosted me for no other reason than that they are nice people and they happen to own a beautiful sailboat. I am lucky to live in a most amazing piece of geography and surrounding it all is the ocean. Whether it sends tiny waves to lap at my toes at low tide or it's blowing up a storm that crashes violently on rocky coves, it's a gift that is priceless beyond compare. I have always been in love with the ocean; as Cousteau put it, the sea has cast its spell on me. The harbors here are full of boats of all kinds. The wind whips through the lines like a mad conductor and produces a cacophony of halyards clanking against a hundred masts that can calm the soul.

There is simply nothing like the feel of the air when there are boats bobbing up and down, gulls calling to each other and the snap of sails can be heard. I've lived all my life with a beach at the end of the street, and I wouldn't have it any other way.

SINK OR SWIM: TALES FROM THE DEEP END OF EVERYWHERE

Something I didn't get to do much of though was sail. I've been on a sailboat exactly twice, and one of those times was a tiny Sunfish on a lake and the ride didn't last long. The first gust of wind sent the boom hurtling towards me and I went Topsiders over tail feathers into Lake Champlain. Sink or swim was not a metaphor on that day; sinking on to a lake bottom of plants and gooey muck was never my plan. After swallowing a few gallons of lake water, I made my way back to the boat, hoisted my soggy butt onto the deck and headed for land.

My very kind friends offered me a ride on their sailboat, to really see what it's like to throw off the bowlines and sail away, which, given the week that had preceded the invite, was exactly what I needed. Not being an accomplished sailor, I had no idea what to bring, so I settled for my beloved St. Patrick's Day Boston Red Sox hat, sunblock and my shades. Opening my home to guests is challenging enough for me, I wanted to make sure that I was a gracious guest as well as hostess, and boat manners might be different than those on land. I hoped that no special attire was expected, like an elegant Ralph Lauren linen tunic or a garish Lilly Pulitzer skirt, because that's just not how I roll.

Weather matters a great deal in sailing, but of course it can't be ordered up with exact specifics. Had that been an option though, the day I spent aboard the Elanore was precisely what would have been requested. Clear skies, low humidity and enough wind to produce gently rolling waves and "happy" sails. That's a technical term by the way, when the wind fills a sail just the right way, it's happy. I loved learning the real terms of sailing, as opposed to the terms I learned from my mother, a Navy veteran, who had the vocabulary of a sailor, but no idea how to behave on a yacht.

There were other technical terms too. It's line, not rope, it's the helm not the steering wheel and the dodger is a canvas canopy not a British pickpocket. There is also something called "dipping the rail" which is when the sailboat rides along with one side dipping precariously into the water, so the waves actually touch the rail. It looks really fun, you know, if it's someone else's boat going by that's doing it. If the boat I was on had been dipping the rail, it's likely I'd have been a very rude guest by leaping up to clutch a life preserver and hollering out a string of Hail Marys.

Manners matter too in sailing, and getting to be with my friends on their boat taught me so much. The etiquette was easily picked up because it's based on consideration for other boaters, their ships, and the environment. While you might own the boat, Mother Nature is a mean beast so you can't forget who is really in charge out there. It's not all Chardonnay and Vineyard Vines, it's so much more. Heading out on a sailboat without a healthy respect for whatever you might encounter is very bad form. There are no street signs, traffic signals or speed limits and a rogue squall can come up anytime and toss you around, but somehow sailors know how to behave in what would be chaos on land.

Each time we passed another boat, everyone smiled and waved at each other and not with just one finger. My friend Laura and her capable husband Captain Chris told me it was likely these same people who would honk at you in traffic, flipping you off while they passed from the right to beat you to a parking space. Something about being out on the water changes things though, in kind of a magical way. I could never have thrown a party quite as elegant as that day on ocean, even if I had a whole houseful of new furniture.

I'm not normally invited to A-list parties either, but on this day, with my friends and a crystal clear sky, I felt like an honored guest and the most fortunate girl in the world.

My children on the other hand have been lucky enough to get invited to so many fun events. They have been to their friends' homes and celebrations and hopefully they have picked up a fairly decent set of manners as a result. My daughter Devin was invited to go swimming one day with a friend. What I hadn't realized is that they weren't going to hop down to the beach but rather they were going to spend the day playing and swimming at the pool of the yacht club her friend's family belongs to, which was just down the street from their home.

She came home sunburned and happy and told me all about going to the snack bar and having frappes and French fries. Immediately I worried that the mom had paid for lunch, and I wanted to offer to pay for her meal. One thing my father taught me was to never be the one whose hand is stuck. Whenever someone offers me a drink or feeds my children, I reach into my pocket to offer to pay.

It's a reflex; no one likes a mooch. It turns out it wasn't necessary; the way it works is that the club keeps track of what members order and then bills it all quarterly. It's technically the same as making brownies or cookies when we have a play date over, but it took me awhile to understand that.

This is not the life I led at her age. When I was 11, if a friend of mine had a swing set that didn't lift up out of the ground when more than one kid got on it that was a big deal. Now my daughter goes on play dates that involve signing for drinks. While my kids have nice friends, who are not snotty, it's sometimes daunting for me. My older son was working on a school project once with a classmate, and when I went to pick him up, he texted me, "Come up the driveway, go past the pool house and take a right at the tennis courts; we're out back." It was like the opening sequence of "Downton Abbey," complete with a yellow lab trotting up the path. It's eye popping sometimes when I look around and see where my children live, but not because of the homes, the boats or the rest of it. It's because I cannot return that level of hospitality. A play date to swim at my house would mean a kiddy pool and a hose. Snacks would be freeze-pops and yogurt cups and there are no tennis courts here, but there have been some wild games of volleyball using the backyard clothesline as a net.

It remains to be seen if that will matter though. I will always maintain an open-door policy at my home. Friends are always welcome. It may be small and a little cramped, but at night I can hear the waves from the beach. Birds float along on the sea breeze and when it rains the scent of sand and salt fills the air. When I hear the seagulls cawing overhead I stop what I am doing, close my eyes for a second and give in to the joy that surrounds me. In these moments I feel the need to tell the universe I am listening and happy to be in my tiny cottage by the sea. I am so close to the centering power of the ocean and so grateful that I get to live in a home that carries so many memories that stopping to acknowledge this gift is a necessity.

The living room might be a mess, and there are no gardens or or grand staircases, but it is our home. It is where we are safe and happy. Parties here might be full of folly, but we like it that way.

12

"If you don't have a dog--at least one--there is not necessarily anything wrong with you, but there may be something wrong with your life."

---Vincent Van Gogh

Anyone who has ever had a dog knows this to be true. Their capacity to love us, to comfort us and to be there every day in their adoring and ever faithful way seems limitless. From the President to the mailman, everyone has something to say about dogs and their devotion to their human companions.

What you don't hear a lot of people saying about dogs is how much of a huge pain in the arse they are. None of the eloquent quotes about dogs and their undying loyalty mention any of the really messy parts of dog ownership. I have had dogs, so I know this. While all of my dogs (Sean, Duffy, Flash, Dingle, Oscar and Penny) have been a part of my family, the last two, Oscar and Penny, are what turned me into a "dog person" or, more specifically, the much more deeply disturbed variant of "pug person."

Pug people are different. Different meaning---well---nuts. It's true. No golden retriever owners go out and buy pearls and a faux mink stole for their dogs, do they? Ever see a black Lab in a baby carriage? Of course not. Those are things that pug owners do. While there is no data on it, pug owners all have at least 7,000 pictures of their dogs. And that's just from last week. There are entire Instagram feeds with just pugs. Pug clothes, pug hats, pug shoes... see what I mean? We pug people are just not normal. And that isn't going to change.

Our first pug, Oscar, was a rescue dog. Believe it or not, someone did actually ask me if he could save people. As if his fat little body could wiggle down a well and rescue a child. Not so much. If an escaped hamster or ferret were menacing you, he would save you from those creatures by gulping up the beast whole. He was also always willing to throw himself on a plate of leftover ham to keep your butt from needing its own zip code.

In the time that Oscar spent with us he gave us unconditional love, there was no doubt of that. If this hadn't been the case, his curly tail would have hit the bricks the first week.

He also gave us every reason to swear off owning any dog that didn't come from a toy store or a taxidermist, but we didn't. Pug people don't give up that easily.

The very first day we had Oscar with us, we were taking him for a walk and noticed that he had picked up something he sniffed out of the bushes and started to eat it. Since we knew he had been abused and not fed enough before coming to us, we expected this, and we looked down to see that he had a ten-dollar bill in his mouth. It was then that we knew he was a good dog, even if he was fat, smelly and slow.

From then on there wasn't much that dog didn't put in his mouth. The old excuse of "the dog ate my homework"? That really happens, only it was a spelling notebook and a backpack hang toy. Add to that Lego mini figs, Barbie heads (yes, JUST the head), paper towels, wrappers of all sorts and an SD memory card from my camera. But give this dog a nice juicy beef bone? Nope, he wouldn't touch that.

In addition to his eating habits, Oscar had allergies. Yes, he had food and seasonal allergies, just like a person would. Every year in late August he'd be at the vet, scratching and sneezing. On a good day pugs breathe in a constant hum like an air conditioner with a bad compressor. In allergy season it's similar to a Harley Davidson missing a tailpipe.

His food was special, he couldn't have certain grains and we couldn't use any soaps or shampoos with raspberries on him or else he would swell up. I always wondered how we'd know, since despite his bizarre eating habits, he was ginormous. Pugs are normally between 12 and 20 pounds full grown. Oscar topped out at 34 pounds at one point, though we did get him down to 29 pounds eventually.

Pugs are a friendly breed and Oscar was no exception. He greeted everyone that walked by our house. Loudly, with a pug howl out the window he snoozed by for 14 hours a day. On a walk, if another person passed us, he would stop and expect to be greeted. If he wasn't he would get a very puzzled look on his face, as if to say "Hey! Hey! I'm Oscar, what's your name?"

And yet for all of this nonsense, the barking, the shedding, the allergies, the weird food issues, the buzz saw breathing, not to mention the unprintable housebreaking issues, Oscar was OUR pain in the arse. I cannot imagine putting up with all of this from anyone or anything but a family dog. Why is that? My own children have caused me to gag and run screaming from the room with their loose teeth and runny noses, but I have wiped up stuff from that dog that probably should have been dealt with by a haz-mat team. When I had a cold, he made me feel better by snuggling behind my knees on the couch and gazing adoringly at me.

His habit of putting anything and everything in his mouth was eventually poor Oscar's undoing. When he was just 8 years old, he ate a Barbie lip-gloss, no doubt because it smelled like ice cream. Just like that, he was gone. People who have not owned pets will think it's ridiculous, but there are not many things that are as painful as having a dog lay his head on your lap, sigh and breathe his last. Owning a dog doesn't make the most sense because they will always break your heart. Why even get a dog if you know that 10-12 years later (if you're lucky) they will leave you sobbing in the parking lot of the vet's office because you can't see to drive home and tell your family he's gone? Oscar was one of a kind, like every other stupid pug, and we still miss him every day.

After a while though, it turned from missing Oscar to missing having a pug. While every family is different, ours wasn't whole without a curly tailed ball of fur making our lives messy, noisy and wonderful. Eventually though, after losing a dog, there comes a time when you need one back in your world. It's different for everyone, but the time definitely comes. Maybe it's returning home to an empty house, with no big slobbery greeting. The wet snout in your face at o'dark-thirty when it's time for the morning walk used to be a nuisance but is now longed for.

Some people believe that we don't choose our pets but rather they choose us. Whether you go to a shelter or a breeder or a rescue group, there is a dog that is meant to be yours. It might seem like a choice, walking past dogs at a shelter or researching breeds, but it really isn't. There is a belief that a dog meant to be in your life will find you and it's absolutely true, at least for us.

The only thing we didn't get with Oscar was the puppy time. He came to us at a year old, so we found a breeder that could work with us and signed up for a puppy. It was almost like waiting for a baby to be born, checking the website every week, to see what was happening. The night our litter was born, we got a text that Lola pug, was in labor and that Max, the dad was pacing nervously. No kidding, we waited up, huddled around the computer refreshing the breeder's website every few minutes to see if the puppies had been born. Newborn pugs look like hamsters for quite some time, but it was still worth the wait. There was no way to tell which pug puppy was ours but around 4 weeks old we got to visit.

There is nothing more moronic and yet thrilling than seeing a litter of squealing baby pugs and knowing your new family member is in this group of stumbling, farting, peeing little fur balls. Leading up to the new arrival our family was focused on naming our girl. We'd decided to go with a girl, because just like humans, pug females are smarter and more fun. We kept lists of names, we jotted them down everywhere and each night at dinner there was hearty debate. Finally, it was decided that our new pug would be named Lulubelle. That's a big name for a little dog, but it's the only one we could remotely agree on.

The day came to go get her and we were amazed at how big she had gotten since we'd first seen her. She weighed a full two pounds and while she was unwilling, she would have fit inside the pocket of my sweater. As we left with her in our arms, there was a penny on the ground. I can't leave a penny on the ground when I see it; it's ingrained in me from the souls of all my dead Irish relatives. That's when it clicked. "Find a penny, pick it up." The dog's name was now Penny and no one wanted to argue with a crazy pug mom, much less a crazy Irish pug mom. My great grandmother was a seanachai, which is Gaelic for "bearer of old lore" but it can also mean "B.S. artist", depending on the situation. There needs to be a story for everything in my family, hopefully with a touch of Irish magic. Find a penny, pick it up, all the day you'll have good luck? It's been a lot longer than a day of good luck with our Penny.

Being so tiny, Penny shivered a lot in those early days, but even doll clothes were too big for her. I grabbed a sock out of the laundry pile, hacked off the foot part and snipped two holes for arms. Presto, a dog sweater! A pug in a sock, it just doesn't get any cuter. I ignored the protests from the sock's owner; the baby was cold, I had to act fast. Not everything she needed was that easy, though, so a shopping trip was necessary. It's possible I overdid it a little, but who doesn't love a pink leash and matching collar?

While we were housebreaking her, she managed to leave a few puddles and piles, but that's part of the deal with any pet. We took her out every half an hour for months, and she finally got the idea. She chewed just about anything she came across, including my toes. At first she slept in a crate at night, and there was a lot of howling and whining. Thankfully the kids stopped that and came to understand that the puppy needs to be safe at night and can't sleep in their beds.

She was the opposite of Oscar in every way. She was tiny; at first she was too small to climb up the one step into our house and had to be carried. That's when she was given her Native American name, "Feet Don't Touch Floor." She was carried around for weeks. She's at her full weight now, a whopping 11 pounds, and she can manage one step, but not more. She doesn't eat everything that she comes across; she has quite a selective palette, but of course she loves cheese as all pugs do.

Now that she's older and has been to puppy obedience training, she's a whole different dog. She can fetch like a pro. In fact it seems that she has an inborn retriever reflex so that anything that is thrown will be brought back. Things that are not thrown will be brought back, even if it's dirty underwear in the hamper, she will bring that back and then wait to be rewarded. Fetch is a never-ending game with her. Whenever anything was thrown around Oscar, if it wasn't food, he'd look at us as if to say, "It's your ball…you get it" and then promptly fall back to sleep.

Penny is a hit wherever she goes and our home now knows the comfort of a four-legged family member. In the days after losing Oscar, I never imagined there could be another pug, much less another dog, for us. He was, and still is, my special boy. He wouldn't fetch or sit or stay. He wouldn't play ball and when he went off the leash he played a game of "puggy keep away" that had us chasing him around like fools until he decided to come back. The one time he slipped out of the house and went on walkabout he only went as far as a neighbor's porch for shelter. It started to rain and he never did like the rain, bless his heart.

Losing him was incredibly difficult, but perhaps he's not completely gone. We do have a pug now, and she makes us all happier, even when she yaps at the mailman, something Oscar never did. Perhaps in each dog that we have, there is the spirit and soul of all of our dogs that came before? I'd like to think so; that way all of my furry children will be with me no matter how deep the water gets.

13

"Simplicity is the keynote of all true elegance"

---Coco Chanel

As a rule, shopping isn't something I've really enjoyed. Friends of mine love to go the mall and wander in and out of the stores, looking at everything. "Retail therapy" is legit, no doubt, it's just never solved anything for me. Getting myself a little treat now and then can be a pick me up, and haunting yard sales for bargains is a favorite hobby, but in general, I am just not a world-class shopper. We all have to do it though, at least at a minimum. Grocery shopping is a must which is why I like to distract myself in the market with the "theater of life" that's usually going on there. There's always something needed for the house, but I would rather chew glass than shop for curtains and rugs and throw pillows (oh my!) I bought paint that had some chemical in it that's probably going to cause me to grow gills at some point, just so I wouldn't have to torture myself picking out colors again. I did that once and no one enjoyed it, not my kids, not the painter and certainly not the poor guy at Home Depot who had to listen to me describe what kind of yellow I wanted because none of 700 different shades of it were exactly what I had in mind.

The worst kind of shopping is for clothes, and that's because I am unable to dress myself in any kind of fashionable way. I read a quote once that said fashion and one's style is about making a statement about who you are without having to actually say anything. That's why it doesn't work for me; talking and writing works for me, picking out clothes does not.

The one exception of course are my shoes. Shoes never make your butt look big. They never shrink in the wash, they don't even need to be dry cleaned. Shoes will be there after Christmas when your jeans have walked off the job after a season of sugar cookies and champagne. A fun pair of shoes will carry you to parties, bring you home safe and never leave you for a new guy. I've gone to concerts, picnics and street festivals and while I may have misplaced my wallet, dropped my phone or lost my car keys, I have never come home without my shoes. They've carried me to some amazing places and I will do the same for them.

Barefoot isn't a look I like and baring anything else isn't an option either. Finding good clothes is a must, even if I'm not very good at it. The alternative is going what my mother used to call "Ballacky booney wild" or naked. No thank you, to do that I'd have to live in some camp and the only thing worse than walking around naked in the woods would be seeing other people walking around naked in the woods. Also, I hate the woods. So, I had to at least find a way to look presentable, if not fashionable. Growing up it was easy; I wore whatever my brother outgrew. Jeans and overalls are pretty basic, and pink was never my color, so it worked for a little while.

Then one year my school pictures came home and it was a wake-up call. There I was in the same ugly plaid sweater that Larry had worn the year before in his school picture.

My parents were mortified thinking that clearly they would be thought of as bad parents for having kids that seemed to share one "good" outfit.

Those pictures somehow never made it onto the mantle; re-takes were done after I'd been dragged to the store and equipped with several things my brother would never have been seen in. Flowery shirts, a knit poncho and bell-bottoms were now mine. It was the 70's after all.

The one thing that did make me happy was that picking out these ensembles was made much easier because some fashion genius back then came up with a matching system. They were called Garanimals. If there was a giraffe on the tag of a shirt, it would match any pair of pants that also had a giraffe on the tag. If they still had a system like that, I would be walking the runways of the world, strutting my perfectly matched bear shirt and bear pants and the zebra dress with the matching zebra sweater. At red carpet events when Ryan Seacrest asked me "Who are you wearing?" I'd just have to glance at the tag and say, "Ryan, this is an antelope, I love it for the clean lines and easy way it lets me move across the Serengeti."

I've mostly just resigned myself to buying clothes in beige, white, navy and black, because the truth is I'm never sure which colors will clash, and which will go. I love bright fuschia pink, and shades of coral, but I think if I wore those two colors together, I might look like I just got off the breakfast shift at Dunkies. Since I'm not required to be all done up in the lastest trends on a day-to-day basis I will usually grab whichever pair of jeans isn't in a heap on the floor, toss on a sweater and be done with it. Sometimes though, the stakes are a little higher, like going to a meeting in an office setting, or lunch at a place without a drive through and this is when I hit the wall. I have absolutely no fashion sense. Zip, zero, zilch. Looking at three pairs of roughly the same style of pin striped slacks and wondering how I'm supposed to know which ones go with a which boring blouse makes me want to give up and wear my pajamas everywhere.

It's not that easy though. Garanimals are a thing of the past and you can't just own clothes in neutral colors. The deep end of the closet can swallow you up if you're not careful, so even for fashion disasters like me, something has to give. My first issue with clothes is the size. I'd like to know what these designers were smoking when they came up with sizes. Vanity sizing? OK, sure, fine. On a good day, I wear a 12. However, if they were to somehow tweak the sizes so that an 8 fits me? That is marketing genius. You bet your sweet arse that's the pair of jeans I'll buy. Doesn't matter how much they cost, they are coming home with me. It's possible I'd put a big sign on the butt that says "SIZE EIGHT" too. That's never happened though and I have a suspicion that like many things in the fashion world, there is some kind of bias that isn't about the fabric. Vanity sizing doesn't seem to apply to the double digits, unless it's a double zero. Once the tags say 10, 12 or 14 it's as if it might as well be sold next to the boat tarps. Newsflash, we up here in the size stratosphere would like a little vanity too.

There's just no rhyme or reason to it. I am challenged enough with math, putting numbers and fashion together is too much. In my closet I have skirts, pants and jeans in sizes 10-14. And they all fit. What fresh hell is this? A foot-long sub is 12 inches. A proper pint of Guinness is 16 ounces. These are standards all over the world and seem easy enough. I'm all for vanity, but I'm tired of feeling like a huge dork when a salesperson says, "What size do you need?" and I'm like a deer in the headlights, finally managing to stammer, "My size. I need MY size, dear God just tell me what size I am!"

The media is no help, either. What possible use are Vogue and Marie Claire when the magazines weigh more than the girls on the cover? How is it that none of these models have snapped a tibia prancing down some set of stairs in four-inch heels? Some of them resemble cake pops because their heads and big hair are so hugely out of proportion to their bodies. I'm shocked they can stay upright, but that's what Red Bull is for I guess.

They are also decades younger than me. I'm pretty tired of seeing teenagers in ads for wrinkle cream and swimsuits. It's creepy. I just can't take fashion advice seriously when the people giving it think there is any outfit that would look good on a walking X-ray. My fashion IQ is so low, I just can't understand the definition of attractive and desirable as the fashion magazines portray it. So with no natural sense of fashion and no wish to emulate the runway models and cover girls that are everywhere, what is the answer? My budget does not allow for a personal stylist. I don't live in "Downton Abbey" where my upstairs maid can fix my hair and bring me the right gloves to go with my dinner gown. I may not be able to pick out my own clothes, but I can get them on my body all by myself once I have them.

As with most things that are important to me, I turn to my friends. When I can't take someone clothes shopping with me, I just snap a picture of something and text it to a friend asking "Do we like this?" Why bother lugging around an iPhone if it can't be of some use? I have even been known to turn to whatever random stranger is nearby, hold something up and ask, "Does this look too much like sofa fabric?" I literally cannot tell sometimes if a piece of clothing looks good on me or if I will see myself on the "People of Wal-Mart" website when I wear it out in public.

Since I am at times a social media junkie, I have also been known to take to Facebook with a quick snapshot of possible outfits and ask, "OK, which one is better?" Then I get several friends weighing in with their advice and suggestions. Most of this is done on a private page I am part of with an amazing group of online friends, most of whom I have never met. Then once I have something decent to wear that has been properly vetted, it might wind up in a photo on my page. Is there a self-help group for people like me? "Hello, I'm Brenda, and I can't dress myself without my imaginary Internet friends."

What I discovered recently, though, was an even better solution to traipsing through the mall with an unwilling but far more fashionable friend or spending hours snapping mirror shots of blouses and skirts: Closet swapping. There's probably some savvy woman who has already started a company that does it, but that's not what I want to do. I was at a friend's house when she happened to be doing some spring cleaning and she said, "Come here, I have to get rid of a few things." Off we went to her closet to weed out what she didn't want anymore.

What an amazing way to shop! No crowds. No poorly lit dressing rooms, just a friend and some brutal honesty. That's the key. If you are going to swap clothes with people, you have to agree ahead of time that no one will get their feelings hurt. This is something you want to do with people that know you really well and can handle the fact that you might not share her taste. Kristen pulled out a dress and said, "You can have this; it's too big for me." Really? She's my friend, so I refrained from cracking the wooden hanger I was holding across the back of her skull and just politely said, "No thanks. I might be a wide arse, but that is one ugly piece of work; did you order it out of the back of the AARP magazine?" I guess in one sense fashion is like friendship, because if you can't count on your friends and a really nice pencil skirt then what is there to count on?

I'm sure this kind of closet swap would work well with a few more women, to give it a little variety. Wine would help, too. At least at the end of the night I'd have spent good times with good friends who know about clothes and what looks good. Maybe I'd even gain a tiny bit of style. A wardrobe consultation would have been a lifesaver the year I showed up at a party wearing a paisley wrap that as it turns out was actually a table scarf. Yes, tables can wear scarves. I learned that the hard way I guess. Now even a piece of furniture can accessorize better than I can. I will admit though, it looked much nicer on the hostess's buffet sideboard than it did over my basic black dress. I really should pay closer attention to what's on the markdown table at Macy's or at the very least try not to shop unsupervised.

Look good feel good right? So what about the rest? Apparently part of being fashionable is what you use on your hair, your skin and your nails. This is where I could easily be a fan of the burqa; there's nothing to worry about with those, they just have holes for your eyes so you don't fall down.

Besides looking good doesn't always mean feeling good. For example, I felt quite fabulous the day I shaved a minute off my mile time at the gym but when I walked by a mirror and caught a glimpse of myself? Wonderful would not describe the feeling I had. It was as if I was looking at something the cat not only dragged in, but pounced on a few times.

I have an amazing hairdresser, so that's not a concern, but the whole idea of a beauty routine is baffling to me. I was looking around at some spa services because maybe there would be a clue there. Lots of people go to spas and get makeovers and manicures and pedicures, so perhaps there was something to learn there. As I perused the services available, some of the ones I found were, well, bizarre.

At one spa, they offered some kind of electromagnetic balancing. Which is what I thought I had done to my tires the last time the car was in the shop, but no, it's a real spa treatment. It requires that a patron go into a room with the "Practitioner" who shows you a handful of Tai Chi moves.

Then, as you lay fully clothed on a massage table, the electromagnetism begins - all without the practitioner having to touch you. Apparently somehow your electro-magnetic field will be more in balance when the practitioner is done chanting. If I put my checkbook on the table, would it get balanced?

Facials are also a big item at spas. Spa employees will put just about any kind of ingredients together and slap them on your face. Some are pretty basic: avocado, cucumbers, tomato peels. To me that's a salad, but hey, if they put it on your face, they can charge you $150 for it and call it "wellness therapy." I just don't see how smearing oatmeal on my face is going to do much good. Some days I would be better off putting the bag the oatmeal came in over my head and calling it "sack therapy."

I recently saw an offering at a trendy spa in New York City that I simply could not believe. It's called the Geisha facial and the key ingredient?

Bird poop. No lie, it's apparently some ancient remedy that Geishas of the past would use when treating someone's troubled skin. It's very specific bird poop though. We are not talking about park pigeons or seagulls. This is nightingale poop and of course using the feces of that particular bird is what makes all the difference.

I found that there are a whole host of other facials too, some that can't really even be described here. Some of them aren't even applied to someone's face or even near their face, so they're more like skin treatments, but honestly, I think I'd rather be a beauty failure than put some of this stuff on any part of me. Some of these procedures use bodily fluids from farm animals and that' just not my style.

Knowing that there are all these radical skin treatments being offered to people makes me stop and wonder who it was who first looked at a nightingale as it flew by and said: "Hey, what if I put the stuff that came out of the back end of that bird on my face?"

And then we have the body wraps. You name any kind of animal, vegetable or mineral and there's probably a spa out there that will wrap you in it. Chocolate body wraps are offered in (where else) the spa at the Hershey Hotel. At other places you can be wrapped in seaweed, herbs, essential oils and probably chips and salsa if that's your thing. These services claim to rid your body of toxins. If I have toxins, how come I'm not deadly? I don't see how wrapping yourself in heated blankets and potpourri is all that different from going outside and rolling around in the compost pile wearing a heavy sweater, but I'm no expert. These treatments also offer "metabolic stimulation." I think that means that after the hemp wrap you have a really bad case of the munchies.

After perusing the hot stone treatments, the "cupping" services, the aromatherapy and all the rest, I think I'm just going to stick with my cold cream from the drug store, basic mascara and whatever lip gloss comes in bubblegum flavor. Simple works for me, anything more would have me in way over my head.

14

"All work is honorable"

---Colin Powell

I heard this quote from a friend of mine and it called to mind discussions I've had about just what constitutes work. And is there honor in everything that we work at?

My first paying job other than babysitting was at a fast food restaurant when I was 15. I wore a bad polyester uniform, ugly shoes and yes, I did have to ask "do you want fries with that?" I learned some important lessons that summer, not the least of which was that while wearing a paper hat and flipping burgers is an honest day's work, it is hard to feel honorable when the rest of your friends are on the beach.

If you are a nanny or a licensed childcare provider, you have a profession. If you clean houses you work. But if you do those same things for your own children is that a job? I personally don't think it is. A job is something you get paid for. Work is everything else you do. We spend a lot of time honoring mothers (and fathers and grandparents) and that is all fine. But every mother I know will say that a good babysitter is worth their weight in gold.

It is real work to raise children. And I firmly believe there is honor in it. I do not believe however, that it's the toughest job in the world. I've had a lot of jobs but "mother" was never one of them. For me personally, while I have had some tough days as a mom, for the most part my hardest day as a mother was still easier than some other things I could name. If your job description includes the possibility of getting shot at or climbing a ladder into a burning building you have a tougher job than I.

I think the person that bags groceries has it harder than I do. I'd last ten minutes in that job. I have trouble getting the bags from the car to the house without dropping something, there is no way I could be trusted not to squash the bread to a pulpy mess under a dozen (and likely broken) eggs.

This year $18.6 billion was spent on Mother's Day gifts; that's an average of $152 per person. Despite a slow economy, that is up $12 per person from last year. But my work as a mom would grind to a halt if there weren't other people doing their jobs well. To name just three: a good plumber, a trusted auto mechanic and a rock star babysitter. They are all essential to keeping me going in this mother gig. But is there a Plumber's Day? Turns out there is, April 25th.

There is also a Childcare Provider Appreciation Day, which really should fall once a week if you ask me.

There are so many others too. When was the last time someone picking up the trash got a "Thank you?" What about the crossing guards at our schools? I know some parents do remember them on the last day of school with a thank you note or a gift card, but what about the other 179 days? How about honoring their work by not racing through the crosswalk inches from their stop sign? Our kids are precious cargo, but how many of them say thank you to the driver when they get off the school bus? Almost none, sadly.

All work is honorable. Most people do not have glamorous jobs however. For every parade the Red Sox or the Patriots are in, for every rolling rally there hundreds of cops and first reponders standing along the way keeping traffic moving and making sure everyone stays safe and sane. Law Enforcement Appreciation Day is usually in May, but saying "Thank you" to a police officer is welcome any day.

I admit, I did not know about any of these special days that acknowledge some of the hard work that makes my life easier. All work is honorable but not all work is honored. That is something I am going to try and be more aware of. And to Mike the plumber, Alan who keeps my car on the road and Kate, a true rock star of childcare, thank you.

What about before we get to the adult part of our lives and can hold down a real job? You almost never hear anyone ask a little kid, "What do you want to be when you grow up?" Personally, I think that's because kids don't play anymore. They take gymnastics and acting classes, they juggle three organized sports at a time. They go to tutoring and trumpet lessons. Then when it's time for the college applications, they do some service project, because it looks good. Kids are building a resume before they can even spell it, but that's a rant for another day.

When I was really little, I wanted to be a nurse. My favorite aunt was a nurse. She had the blue cape and the white cap and she was amazing. She even got me my very own custom made nurse's dress, a real cap and gave me her nurse's watch, which was magical to me with it's glow-in-the-dark dial. She died when I was 7 and without her, I lost the drive and direction. It's probably just as well; science was never an easy subject for me and if someone has a phlegmy cough, I puke.

The next career that interested me was writing for a newspaper. I edited the junior high yearbook, the high school yearbook and edited the Headlight, back in my time at Marblehead High School. Going off to college I was certain that journalism was for me. For whatever reason, it wasn't. I dropped the journalism major, graduated with a BA in English and set off on the first of what has seemed like 700 different jobs.

That's the thing; they were jobs not careers. Once the children came along, duking it out in the field of federal law enforcement, investigating unions and racketeering just wasn't fun anymore. Being a mom was what I wanted most, but for me, it wasn't a job. To call being a mom a job is giving short shrift to all that goes into being a parent. It's definitely work; it's difficult and demanding and it's messy, but I never considered it a job. I considered it something much more. It didn't just pound out a small screaming human, I had to make sure I didn't kill it, lose it or otherwise screw it up and that is a lot to do. Way more work than any job I ever had.

Eventually though, the kids went to school and I wanted back in to the paid working world. In the space of about 10 years I was an airline reservationist, a preschool aide, a waitress, a mystery shopper (yes, that's a real thing) and a web designer. From those jobs I moved into travel and tourism and spent time working for TripAdvisor and America Online on content and marketing. In every job, writing was required and I loved sitting down and cranking out copy or writing a report.

I honestly had no idea where I was going though. There was no real goal other than not to starve to death. When people tell me about the jobs they've had and what they liked best there are some really good stories. One friend from the whitest town in the world got her first job out of college at a video company that did work for Black Entertainment Television. She met Louis Farrakhan and Al Sharpton but she also met David Bowie and Smokey Robinson and had dance parties in the control room to the music videos they played. It was an about-face from her upbringing and insanely fun.

My friend's job stories convinced me that we all eventually find what we love to do. Maybe along the way there will be jobs that have to be done to pay the bills, but keeping the engines running on what's important to you is key. I gave up journalism when I was 19. Twenty-five years later, I was hired as a columnist for a newspaper. Looking back at my path? It's all twisty-turny like that kid in the Family Circus comic strip, but finally it's a career, it's what I love and it makes me happy. The not starving to death thing is an issue though. Here's a tip: don't go into writing for the money, it's like having a kid. If you don't love it, it will get ugly fast.

If you don't know what you want to be, then just be you. Try everything; even jobs that sound awful might not be so bad. If you don't like what you're doing, do something else. It's like Dr. Seuss said, "You have brains in your head. You have feet in your shoes. You can steer yourself any direction you choose. Things may happen and often do to people as brainsy and footsy as you!"

Once your career is in motion though, it's the last place you want to sink, because it's not easy finding the right place and the right kind of work. What's going to motivate you to work hard? Ask 50 people that question and you will get 50 answers. Maybe more than 50 because there's almost always more than one reason why we do the things we do. Motivation often depends on the task as well.

There's no escaping the fact that there are things in life we have to do, so perhaps motivation is a moot point. We work because we have to pay the bills; we clean the house because we don't want to be overrun by dust bunnies. Those things are pretty simple, and most of us don't put that much thought into them. But if our jobs, homes, kids and other responsibilities become just a big to-do list, then what keeps us in the game? What makes us want to work harder and do more? It can't just be a desire to stay above water.

In the average job there are usually well-defined responsibilities and criteria to be met. There are benefits and salaries and the like. However, almost no one I know is motivated solely by those factors. Sure, people like bonuses and raises, but that's only a small part of it. Recently, in my job there was a last minute assignment I was asked to do. My regular work was done, this was something not normally required. Sure, there was payment involved but that's not why I rearranged some plans to get it done. I could have easily said no. I did it because my boss said to me, "I would really appreciate it if you could help out with this." Are there any more magical words than "I appreciate it?" Too many times we forget to let people know that they matter. In a business environment, some companies think payroll takes care of that. Not entirely. A paycheck is only part of what keeps employees working hard. Outside of a business environment, it's even more important. Who tells a stay-at-home parent that they matter? Almost no one, in my experience. Even fewer people tell an adult child who is caring for an elderly or ailing parent that their choice matters.

Everyone needs to know that what they do is appreciated in some way. That's the thing about motivating people; sometimes all it takes is a few well-chosen words. Words mean things. They can be what keeps a person heading for shore instead of giving up.

The expression "going the extra mile" is part of every performance review it seems and it's not just a running term. My goal in any job has always been to give 110%, even if that's not mathematically possible. Every now and then though, I will question if it's worth it. If I put in a ton of extra effort will there be a raise or a bonus? Will that corner office be mine, will the boss put me on the really good project that involves a trip to New Orleans? No, probably not.

That isn't how going the extra mile is supposed to work. It's supposed to pay off in intangible ways like feeling personally satisfied, or perhaps earning some good karma. The business world isn't one where you normally hear about karma though, so it's hard to decide how much to give.

It's all business. It's a numbers game; nothing more, nothing less. A pound of hamburger is $5. If I walk into a store with $5, that's how much burger I can buy. It's a retail store; expecting more is foolish and regularly handing out more than what is paid for is a bad business plan. Simple, right? Do only what you're paid to do, pay only for what you actually get. Not always. At some point there's a choice has to be made. It's like the movie "The Wizard of Oz" where Glinda asks Dorothy, "Are you a good witch, or a bad witch?" Dorothy was rocking the red shoes, which is why I like her so much. She made the choice to help others, and I try to go a little further down my own yellow brick path when I can too. There will be times when all it results in are blisters and bad news, but since I have some really nice shoes, you can find me putting some extra miles on them whenever possible.

15

"Only by weathering the greatest storms can we appreciate the most beautiful skies."

---Tyler Knott Gregson

It's definitely true that nothing is permanent, not the good things but not the bad either. This too shall pass is something a friend always said, no matter what it was I was bitching about. Honestly, I found it completely unhelpful. Of course it would pass, everything does. In the meantime how do we just keep going? Are all these quotes about what to do and how to feel really helpful? No, not always. Words are my thing; they are my currency and my go to. I can't draw or paint. I can't sing or dance, I can't build things or do math that involves numbers higher than 21 and I really suck at parallel parking. But give me some words and there will be a story, a memory and hopefully a laugh. Some words though, are just not helpful.

Phrases or sayings that invoke God or a Higher Power for something mundane are really of no use. This is thin ice because the subject of religion is very personal. I'd rather cut off my iPhone access than offend anyone, but in my opinion, one's belief in God, the Bible, Judaism, Buddha or whatever else is far too big to be applied to the little things. I would much rather have God be with those who are truly having a major need in their lives than be my co-pilot on stupid errands like that old bumper sticker says. Is God in your car? Well for Christ's sake (literally) pull over so you two can talk. God, however you define Him/Her or Them, is much larger and worthy of more than just riding shotgun. I have walked by a family in a theme park, with their heads bowed in prayer and heard them ask Jesus to grant them short lines on Space Mountain and the Dumbo ride. On the one hand, this family had an amazing gift, that of faith, and they were not afraid to show it in public. Kudos to them. On the other, I believe Jesus might be too busy to worry about ride lines, at least I surely hope so.

Sayings that don't really solve the problem or offer anything concrete are useless to me as well. Even if all a quote gives you is a mental picture that eases your mind it's worthwhile, but so many people go around offering platitudes that just don't help at all. They mean well and it's hard sometimes to know just what to say to someone who is hurting, but phrases like "Everything happens for a reason," "Stay the course" and "When one door closes, a window opens" are useless. Windows? Oh please, shut the... front door on that crock. Everything happens for a reason? OK, and then what? You know when I heard most of these overused phrases? When my mother killed herself four months after my father died.

Perhaps I was just too deep in my grief and anger to appreciate that people had good intentions, but trust me, if someone you care about loses someone? Don't say any of those things. No one likes hearing these fortune cookie lines and it's not comforting, ever. Also, when you say something that is painfully obvious, it makes you sound painfully ignorant. Stuff like "You only live once" and "Tomorrow is another day?" Once? You mean we don't get five more tries at this life thing? The world is not ending right this second? Come on now, no one needs to be told that.

Another awful way to use words is to make huge generalizations that paint whole groups with a wide brush that's not even close to accurate. You want to talk nails on a chalkboard? "Boys will be boys" or anything

SINK OR SWIM: TALES FROM THE DEEP END OF EVERYWHERE

like it makes me want to smack someone. Except then I might hear that I "fight like a girl" and that would end badly for sure. In all honesty, the words "typical man" have crossed my lips and not in a nice way, but it's still not a good idea to lump entire groups all together with trite phrases that don't mean anything. There are a thousand different kinds of women, men, mothers, fathers, teachers, plumbers, bikers and engineers. To ignore that is to miss a huge chunk of knowledge and there's no one alive who couldn't use more of that.

One of my favorite sayings to describe something came from my very wise friend and fellow Irish woman, Catherine. She was kind enough one summer to invite me to her parents' home by the sea on Long Island. Her father had purchased land and built the summer cottage in the Hamptons, long before the Hamptons were the polo playground of the rich and obnoxious. The house faces Three Mile Harbor and sitting on the deck we could have morning coffee and watch the boats go by. Her father, Martin Quinn, a World War II veteran and member of the Greatest Generation called it his "million dollar view" and it was.

The bay flowed into a pond that the kids could swim in and that became an afternoon staple along with vodka gimlets and ice cream after supper. One day I took her two girls and my boy to the pond while Catherine nursed her youngest. They all leaped into the pond and almost immediately I could tell something wasn't right. It was high tide and this created deeper water, and on windy days, a bad undertow. In no time, her girls were in the middle of the pond, unable to get back in and my boy was struggling too. I hollered like an anciet Irish banshee for Catherine who came racing down. We got every body back safely, but it was one of the scariest moments of my life, by far.

Ever since, when things are not going well for me, when I am the one in the deep end and struggling for shore, I call Catherine and without having to explain or apologize I say, "It's high tide at the pond." She always knows what to say. While seeing the kids in trouble that day was a one-off and will hopefully never be repeated, the truth is that it's high tide at the pond twice a day. Every day. There's no getting away from a high tide, and it can really screw up your day if you're not careful.

A lot of times, when these days come and I am in over my head, my first instinct has been to stay home, binge watch bad television and hate the world. For the record, it's never been the right solution; it's never helped. What's better is to go out and be in the world, as hard as that is sometimes. It's a guarantee that we are all going to have a bad day from time to time. We might even get a few in a row, one after the other. Everyone's go-to solution is different though. It's easy to say to say someone, "Just keep swimming" as if they were some bright blue Disney fish. It's hard to keep swimming sometimes, damn hard. Sink or swim, right?

Actually no, there's another option. Tread water. Seriously, just like that whole "what doesn't kill you makes you stronger" nonsense there are more options than something being deadly or empowering, more outcomes than being safe on shore or at the bottom of the sea. Treading water is sometimes the best you can do, but it's a victory nonetheless. Here is something else I've come to realize. Unless you are the President and there is some national crisis going on, you can end any day you don't like, anytime you want. Just call it over. Done, finished, the end. We get a new day every twenty-four hours. The sun comes back up and while there will be more high tides it's another chance. If you only manage to stay in one place for a bit, not backsliding, but not moving forward, so what?

No one stays in one place forever. Pretty soon your arse falls asleep and you need to move it and you're right back in the game. You're not stuck; you're resting. Treading water is much like the advice Elizabeth Taylor gave about bad days when she said, *"Pour yourself a drink, slap on some lipstick and pull yourself together."* It doesn't sound like it would help, but it does. While not everyone would choose lipstick and a glass of wine, sometimes something else comes around and that's all it takes.

One dark winter day, I was stuck inside with my cranky kids, a mountain of laundry, a backlog of work and I was just done with it all. The parts of my life that always made me happy just weren't doing it. My tiny cottage by the sea was a mess of toys and dirty dishes. My children were going at it like two raccoons in a trash barrel and nothing I did for my job was right. After the third email chewing out of the day from a boss I hope I never have to speak to again and upon whom I wish an embarrassing gastrointestinal condition that results in room-clearing flatulence and an itch he can't scratch in public, I headed down to the cellar to at least attempt to throw in some wash. I was trying to stay afloat by keeping busy, that's supposed to work, right?

It's important to note here that I have what I refer to as my "lottery house" designed in my head. It doesn't resemble my actual home in any way. It will have big rooms, bay windows that actually overlook a bay and some kind of magical floor system that cleans itself. One of its main features will be a laundry room, with two washers and two dryers, piped in music and a door that opens to a sunny patio with a clothesline. My actual laundry area is a dark, damp space with no sunlight and no patio. If it was possible, I would put the washer and dryer somewhere else in my house, but it's just not.

So, I'm furiously sorting the clothes out in this cave-like space and a terrible realization hits me like a rogue squall. I didn't want to be there anymore. I didn't want to be anywhere. I just wanted to be gone. It's something I couldn't even articulate at the time, nor can I now, but I wanted out. Anything had to be better than where I was; if I could have magically poofed away into thin air I would have. That's when I heard the television. Normally I tuned it out since in those days it was always on some kiddy show with talking sponges, puppets or cartoon karate chopping turtles.

On this day, loud and clear I could hear Ernie, from Sesame Street. I've always been a fan of Sesame Street, but my kids had outgrown it too fast for me. Ernie was singing about being able to go to amazing places and see things like dinosaurs and hear jungle lions roar. The song was so clear in my head that day Ernie could have been standing right next to me. He sang about wanting to visit the moon, and look down at the Earth from up there but then he'd miss all his friends and family. He decided while it might be nice to visit, for one afternoon, he just would not want to live on the moon. He wanted to dive deep under the ocean, but sea creatures couldn't be his real family. This orange puppet had the words I couldn't come up with.

Seems pretty nuts doesn't it? I know. Much like high tides though, and big waves and swirling undertows, moments come when they come and just cannot be planned or predicted.

We never know when we're about to get Maytag'd by a wicked wave, just as we never know when that little but of help is going to show up. Sure, it was puppet on a kid's show, but it was just what I needed to hear. It didn't fix everything instantly of course. It didn't make me immediately happy, it didn't snap me out of my mood and I didn't dance back up the stairs and bake cookies. I treaded water though for a good long time actually. I stuck around, in the same spot, but still afloat. Then, slowly, I was swimming again.

It wasn't my last time being in the deep end, but that's because like my friend pointed out, there's a high tide twice a day. There could be a deep end just around the corner, but there could also be a good friend to lead you to shore, a fun song to remember while you tread water and finally, sand between your toes when you get back to shore.

There's no way we can avoid getting in over our heads now and then. No ocean is calm all the time, because that isn't what an ocean is supposed to be. Waves might take you down, but they always beat incessantly towards the shoreline. Every high tide recedes. Storms will come and toss us around, that's a given. It might seem like a wonderful dream to just

SINK OR SWIM: TALES FROM THE DEEP END OF EVERYWHERE

float through life, never having to struggle against the current, but how would you ever get anywhere? The skies will clear though and the waves will calm down. Pour yourself a nice drink, throw on some fun shoes and go on your way. Cheers!

Made in the USA
Middletown, DE
14 March 2021